Background to Breckland

BY

H. J. MASON AND A. MCCLELLAND

ILLUSTRATED BY JASON PARTNER

PROVIDENCE PRESS

First Published March 1994
Providence Press, 38B Station Road,
Haddenham, Ely, Cambridgeshire.

ISBN 0-903803-27-5

CONTENTS

The War Memorial, Thetford Road, near Elveden

FOREWORD

Thetford Forest Park attracted over one and a half million visitors last year and yet because of the vast area that it covers it never seems crowded, other than when special events are being staged. Most of the access is now provided by Forest Enterprise, the leisure, recreation and educational division of the Forestry Commission.

Thetford Forest covers 20,000 hectares of woodland, the first trees were planted in 1922. It now produces 200,000 cubic feet of timber annually and has a rotation of clear felling and replanting. Since harvesting began the Commission has exploited opportunities to improve habitats for wildlife, to enhance the beauty of the forest by planting broad-leaved trees in sensitive areas and to improve leisure and recreational facilities. In spite of timber production being the prime reason for the forest, access is widely permitted and a visitor centre has been established at High Lodge.

Regrettably the Forestry Commission is threatened with privatisation which in our opinion would be detrimental to conservation and to the public enjoyment of this wonderful national asset created by the faith and imagination of the pioneer planters in the early twentieth century. Our book is written in the context of facilities currently available and in the hope that Forest Enterprise will be able to continue to develop the excellent work it is doing.

Heathland is the closest reminder we have of what Breckland was like after the earliest inhabitants had cleared the natural woodlands. There are good examples of this habitat which can be visited and where unusual and rare plants and birds can be found.

Breckland will face threats from developments such as a forest-fuelled power station and large scale charcoal production. Whilst these might be good for its commercial future, any changes that are allowed must be sensitively integrated into the countryside.

It is our hope that this book will give the reader an appreciation of how this unique area has evolved and encourage exploration of its historical remains, wildlife, forestry, farming and recreational facilities.

Before walking into the forest and heaths it is wise to give a little thought to appropriate clothing. This is because there are ticks which can transmit Lyme Disease. The chances of this happening are extremely rare but anyone who is concerned should wear long trousers tucked into socks during the period from April to October when the ticks are most active. A very good leaflet is available on the subject.

Leaflets issued by Breckland District Council give information about Breckland Traditions, Churches, Heaths and Meres, Thetford and Wildlife.

The Ordnance Survey Landranger Map 144 covers most of Breckland, but Maps 143 and 155 are also useful. We would like to acknowledge the help and encouragement that we have received from many people in the preparation of this book.

Jim Mason   *Anne McClelland*

February 1994

Chapter One

FEATURES OF BRECKLAND

Breckland occupies an ill defined area of south Norfolk and north Suffolk. It stretches from near Bury St Edmunds in the south, almost to Attleborough in the east, to Swaffham in the north and merges with the Fens from Methwold to Lakenheath in the west.

The word 'breck' is probably derived from an old Norwegian word 'braec' meaning 'land newly broken for settlement'. The land was broken for a few years for cropping and then allowed to revert to its former state (which in Breckland was then heath) to regain fertility before being cultivated again. Heathland is the most typical feature of the area but is now greatly diminished due to afforestation and the development of farming practices which have made continuous cultivation possible.

Scots Pine trees are the most striking feature of Breckland where they are seen as single rows or in groups or in large forest blocks. Outside of the forest they were first planted as wind breaks at the time of Enclosure, from 1768 onwards. They line roads and the edges of fields and their branches and trunks are often twisted with age.

Three rivers, the Wissey, the Little Ouse and the Lark cross Breckland and in their shallow valleys most villages are situated. Flint is the only really durable building stone found in the area and it is used extensively on older buildings such as churches, farmsteads and cottages. Some streets in Brandon and Thetford still have a preponderance of flint houses in them. The less durable chalk clunch can be seen in a few village buildings. After the mid-nineteenth century bricks could be easily and cheaply brought in by rail and were much more widely used from then onwards.

Underlying Breckland is a layer of chalk, which is up to 400 metres thick in some parts of Norfolk. The chalk was deposited during the Cretaceous Period which lasted from about 100 to 65 million years ago. At that time, up to 80 per cent of the present land surface was flooded. The climate was much warmer then than it is now and the melt water from the polar ice cap caused a great ocean, up to 270 metres deep, to form.

In the warm waters there were myriads of minute unicellular plants and animals consisting mainly of chalk. These creatures were so small that if 20 were clustered together they might just be visible to the naked eye. When they died they gradually sank to the bottom to form a chalky ooze. The particles which settled became compressed by the weight of water above them and ultimately by the weight of the accumulated chalk. The process of accretion was extremely slow, having been estimated at about 5 mm. in 1,000 years.

The waters also contained shellfish which added to the chalk but there are surprisingly few fossils found in it. This is probably due to the slow build-up of chalk from the ooze. The larger shells would have disintegrated before they were covered except in such cir-cumstances where they fell into holes created by burrowing worms, or were buried by fish swimming near the bottom, stirring up the ooze which, when it eventually settled, engulfed the dead shellfish. As a consequence of the slow build-up, fossils separated by only a few centimetres would have been creatures which lived thousands of years apart.

The changes at the end of the Cretaceous Era were so dramatic that dinosaurs became extinct and mammals gradually began to evolve. The great chalk ocean receded, more land appeared, and continental masses began to separate. The infant Atlantic Ocean formed and slowly expanded as the continents drifted apart. Into the sub-tropical sea which formed, rivers flowed carrying mineral material. This was deposited in the deeper water as clay. Much of the sediment which makes up southern England dates from this period.

It is thought that much of the East Anglian chalk was uplifted by the force of the earth's movements and thus remained exposed above the water level until the much later onset of the Ice Ages.

The Ice Ages were of major significance in the formation of

Breckland as it is today. The glaciers brought particles of minerals which made up the soils and 'drift' deposits over the chalk. The early geologists used the term 'drift' as they thought the material was carried by glaciers and deposited where they melted. The term used now is 'boulder clay'. It is very variable in composition and its nature depends on where it was picked up by the glaciers which pushed south with steady but irresistible force. During this movement, some of the boulder clay was dropped from the base of the ice mass but most accumulated within it. When the climate warmed up again, the ice melted, leaving behind all the material that it had been carrying.

There were two glaciations which were thought to have had a major effect on the Breckland area. The first of these, known as the Anglian Glaciation, occurred from about 350,000 to 200,000 years ago. It covered the whole of East Anglia as far south as the Thames valley. Breckland would have been subjected to the scouring and erosive effect of the movement of the glacial ice. Valleys were gouged out and varying amounts of boulder clay were left as the ice retreated. Rivers flowing from the melting ice began to re-sort the boulder clay, carrying larger stones which were deposited as gravels on river terraces, while finer materials such as sands and silts were carried further down the valleys in the slower running water.

During the inter-glacial period other natural agents also helped to re-sort and re-distribute some of the drift material. Inter-seasonal periods of frost broke down the constituents into smaller particles which could be blown to form sand dunes and deserts, or carried in rivulets and streams.

The last glaciation to affect Breckland, the Devensian, occurred about 70,000 years ago and lasted for about 60,000 years. The continuous ice sheet only came as far south as the present North Norfolk coast but it had a profound effect on the Breckland area which was in a zone of permafrost. During this period the land was more or less permanently frozen to a depth of several tens of metres. The summer sunshine was sufficient to raise the temperature high enough for a slight thaw to take place on the surface. The water produced, unable to soak away, either became trapped in a depression on the surface to form a small lake or bog, or ran downhill where there was a gentle slope and no obstruction.

In areas where the chalk was near the surface, small fissures were created by the water dissolving the chalk. Water expands by about 9 per cent of its volume when it freezes. This creates a tremendous force as is well demonstrated when ice fractures a water pipe or lifts the top off a milk bottle when the milk (which is mainly water) freezes. The water trapped in small fissures in the chalk froze each winter and made the cracks very slightly wider and deeper every year. Over the centuries the fissures became enlarged and when the ice receded they were filled with drifting sand and silt. In this way polygons of soil were created. They can still be seen on some ploughed land in the spring before there is a crop cover, and in the variations in vegetation on heathland.

On sloping ground the cracks developed down the slope and have a similar effect on the soil and vegetation. On some heaths, the plants which can tolerate acidity grow on the soil in the cracks where there is no lime, and calcium-loving plants grow in between where chalk is much nearer the surface.

Scattered around Breckland are a considerable number of small, usually round ponds called 'pingos'. Pingo is an Eskimo word meaning a small hill of ice, which describes perfectly the way in which these ponds originated during a permafrost period. They may have arisen from an underground spring becoming frozen near the surface but unable to penetrate it. Gradually, more water was added until a cone of ice formed. Some of the earth (perhaps all) fell by gravitation to the edges of the ice cone into a bank surrounding the ice. When the ice melted, an embanked hollow filled with water remained as a pingo.

Much larger expanses of water, called meres, are also unexpectedly found in this otherwise dry and arid area. Some are man-made, e.g. Thompson Water and Stanford Water. Others, such as Langmere, Fowlmere, Ringmere and the Devil's Punchbowl, are natural and have no visible inlet or outlet.

The natural meres are depressions, possibly arising from the underlying chalk being dissolved and eroded to form a cavity. The level of the water in these meres is dependent upon the level of the permanent water table in the subsoil. The fluctuating level reflects the amount of rain (or lack of it) over a number of years. After they have dried out, as in 1992, a few centimetres of rain has no effect.

Heavier than normal rainfall is needed before water reappears, a process which could take several months or years.

Fears have been expressed that the aquifers in the chalk are being lowered (perhaps depleted) by the abstraction of water from deep boreholes. This may be a contributory factor, but there are good historical records of these fluctuations which occurred long before the water in the chalk was being exploited for domestic use.

Ringmere, situated on East Wretham Heath, a reserve run by the Norfolk Naturalists Trust, is circular with steep sides and when full has an area of nearly three hectares. In 1724 it was described as 'a remarkable cavity, in the form of an amphitheatre .... with a uniform descent on every side to the arena...there was not in the latter end of October, a drop of water in it, which the wet summer must have filled if it had been a pond'. In July 1830 it was said to be 'so full of water that it overflowed the Hockham road, the water being for several weeks two feet deep on the road.' By September 1835 it was 'entirely without water' but by 1844 'it again overflowed the Hockham Road to a greater degree than in 1830 and so it remained until September of this year.' It was dry for two years in 1901 and 1902 but again overflowed the Hockham Road in 1950.

In 1724-25 Fowlmere was dry, full in 1834 and dry again in 1859-62 when oats and wheat were successfully grown there. It was cropped again in 1901 but the root crops in 1903 had to be harvested by men standing knee-deep in water.

Langmere, a 5 hectare mere, also on East Wretham Heath, has shown similar fluctuations in water level, and in 1988 it was at the highest level ever recorded. In February of that year, a bird-hide overlooking the mere was completely flooded but by July the water level had begun to recede and a few years later the mere was completely dry.

The Devil's Punchbowl (Croxton) is one of the smallest meres (0.5 hectares) and is easily accessible from a Forestry Commission picnic area off the Harling Drove. In 1990 when it was completely dry, there was still some water in Fowlmere, on the opposite side of Harling Drove and it did not dry up until nearly two years later. There was some water in the meres again in early 1994 following a wet autumn in 1993.

Micklemere, which is fed by a small stream and is not therefore

Devil's Punchbowl, May 1989

Devil's Punchbowl, May 1992

subject to such wide fluctuations in water level, had a duck decoy with ten pipes built around it during the early part of the nineteenth century. This indicates then, as now, the importance of the Breckland meres for waterfowl, as the decoy would have been expensive, both to construct and maintain.

When in use, ducks were enticed into one of the pipes, usually with the help of a small, fox-like dog. Along the edge of one side of the water of each pipe, there were hurdles made from reeds. These were placed at an angle to the water and there was a gap between each. When the decoy man judged there were enough ducks near the entrance to a pipe, he took his dog along a screened path to start work. The dog was trained to go round and round the hurdles and the ducks were attracted by curiosity towards it as it alternately appeared and disappeared. The decoy man watched from behind a screen and as the ducks moved towards the pipe he whistled the dog, which then began to circle round the next hurdle further away from the entrance. After this had been repeated a few times, there would be enough ducks in the pipe for the decoy man to come out from behind his screen to frighten them into flying down it. The pipe was constructed with a curve so that the ducks could not see that they were flying into a blind alley eventually ending in the net from which there was no escape. The ten pipes were necessary as ducks could be caught from all areas of the mere no matter where they were drifting. Also the decoy man could always work downwind to ensure that there was a minimum chance of the ducks detecting his presence by scent. There was a ready market for the ducks and operating a decoy of this nature was very profitable when wildfowl were plentiful.

The water levels of man-made meres fluctuate far less than the natural meres as they are fed from streams. During the dry years 1989 to 1992 the level of Thompson Water fell very little unlike Cockley Cley lake which began to dry up in September 1991 and by January 1992 it was completely dry, killing thousands of fish and destroying, temporarily, a valuable wildfowl habitat. By the end of March 1992 it was again full of water and the wildfowl had returned, although recolonisation by plants and fish takes far longer.

All the features of Breckland - the chalk, clay and sandy soils, the polygons, pingos, flint mines, heaths, pines, and the unusual indigenous flora and fauna - combine to make an area not only full of interest and beauty but also one that is unique.

Breckland pines

Chapter Two

THE HISTORY OF BRECKLAND

The first inhabitants of Breckland were the hunters and foragers of the Paleolithic (Old Stone) Age, whose flint choppers and flake-tools have been discovered near Barnham. Excavations in the area in the 1970s and from 1989 to 1990 have enabled these tools to be dated to about half a million years ago, making the site the oldest one in Britain. The Neolithic (New Stone) Age people found the lightly-wooded, sandy soils of Breckland easy to clear and cultivate with ploughs in which flint axe-heads were used as shares. For two or three years crops of emmer wheat or barley were grown on a piece of land. It was then rested and grazed by cattle and sheep to prevent regeneration of woodland, but when the community moved on, bracken, heather, gorse and mosses grew on the cleared land which became heath.

When a Neolithic farmstead, covering one and a half hectares near Hurst Fen, Mildenhall, was excavated, arrowheads, querns and fragments of pots with rounded bases were found. To understand about these early Breckland people visit Grimes Graves, the site of their intensive mining activities. In the mine open to the public it is possible to climb down a steel ladder and stand on the floor of a shaft dug out about 4,000 years ago and crouch down to look along galleries spanning out from the centre. It is amazing to think of the effort expended to extract flint in this first industrial site in Britain.

There are two ancient trackways in Breckland. The Icknield Way links Stonehenge and Avebury in Wiltshire with Grimes Graves. It gives its name to the villages of Icklingham and Ickburgh and, until the Little Ouse was bridged in the seventeenth century, was the principal route into Thetford. Harling Drove runs for fourteen miles through Breckland, from Blackdyke at Hockwold to Roudham and thus links the Fens to the Peddars Way. It passes close to Fowlmere, Langmere and Ringmere which all provided watering places for the herds of cattle and sheep which at one time were driven along it.

Bronze Age settlements at Lakenheath and West Row near Mildenhall were of circular post houses and have yielded pottery, worked flints and seeds of grain and flax. Round barrows containing Bronze Age burials are very numerous, though often disguised by having had Scots Pines planted on top of them in the eighteenth and nineteenth centuries! Tutt Hill to the west of Rushford, Mickle Hill near the Devil's Punchbowl and Hut Hill on Knettishall Heath are round barrows.

There is an Iron Age riverside site at Micklemoor Hill near East Harling and a farmstead buried beneath the Anglo-Saxon village of West Stow. The only known Iron Age fort in Breckland is at Barnham, dates from the second century BC and has a double rampart and ditch.

A well-known Roman feature of Breckland is the Peddars Way,

Round Barrow, Icklingham

now a long-distance footpath from Knettishall to Holme-next-the-Sea, on the North Norfolk Coast. It crosses Breckland almost in a straight line and the embanked agger is visible along some of its length. Names such as Woodstreet Farm and Thorpe Street point to the existence of other Roman roads.

The Iceni tribe inhabited Breckland at the time of the Roman invasion (AD 43). Iceni weapons, parts of their chariots and horse harnesses have been found at Elveden, Santon, Lakenheath and Icklingham. The triple- ditched enclosure at Thetford, with three circular wooden buildings within it, was probably a religious centre for the tribe.

The Romans made a treaty with the Iceni which lasted until AD 61 when Boudicca, leader of the tribe, led a rebellion which resulted in the burning of the Roman towns of Colchester and St Albans and an attack on London before the Iceni were defeated by Suetonius Paulinus in a battle whose site has not been positively identified. With peace restored, agriculture developed and market centres were established at Icklingham and Mildenhall. Roman farming estates and villas have been found at Eriswell, Mildenhall, Lackford, Brettenham and along the valley of the Little Ouse from Hockwold to Santon.

Evidence of the adoption of Christianity by the Romano-British comes from the archaeological finds at Icklingham of lead cisterns inscribed with the words 'chi-ro', 'alpha' and 'omega'. There is a possibility that these were used as fonts for baptism.

The most well-known Roman remains found in Breckland is the Mildenhall treasure which consists of thirty-four objects of almost pure silver, now in the British Museum. It includes bowls, embossed silver dishes, goblets, ladles, plates and spoons. In 1979 near Gallows Hill, Thetford, another hoard of Roman gold and silver was discovered. It consists of twenty-two gold rings, bracelets , necklaces and pendants and thirty-three silver spoons. None appears to have been used and some were unfinished but were evidently buried, like the Mildenhall treasure, at the end of the fourth century.

The reconstructed Anglo-Saxon village at West Stow gives a vivid idea of what such a settlement was like, not only here but in many places in Breckland. Excavations from 1965 to 1972 revealed the pits and post-holes of buildings used from about AD 420 to AD

650. One family grouping of houses and a hall has been rebuilt using the same sort of materials and tools the Saxons would have used. The taped guide to the village gives an imaginative picture of life in the hall. Sitting on a bench and watching smoke rise to the roof from the central hearth you can listen to the saga of Beowulf, just as the Saxons gathered and were entertained through winter nights.

At Lackford, near West Stow, was an Anglo-Saxon cemetery with over a thousand cremations in urns. Another such cemetery has been found at Illington, with 212 urns. At Brandon, a site occupied from the seventh to the ninth century has revealed timber buildings, one of which was aisled and was probably the hall. Pottery from the Continent, coins and a gold plaque inscribed with an eagle have been found there.

Anglo-Saxon place-names are much in evidence, especially around Thetford. They include 'ham' meaning homestead as in Brettenham, Wretham and Hockham; 'ton' meaning enclosure, as in Tottington, and Santon; 'mere' meaning pond, hence Ringmere, Fowlmere and Langmere. 'Burgh' a fortified settlement is represented by Ickburgh and 'ingas' the followers of, by Weeting, Cressingham and Harling.'Ford' is Anglo-Saxon for a river crossing and occurs frequently with Culford, Lackford, Langford, Lynford and Thetford as examples.

The Danes attacked Eastern England in AD 841. In AD 870 King Edmund was killed by the Danish invaders and was buried at Bury St Edmunds. That year, the Danish army spent the winter in Thetford which was by then a thriving commercial centre producing ornaments, ironware, woollen goods and pottery. It is possible that Ringmere was the site of a battle between the Danes and the Saxons in AD 1010. By the time of the Domesday Survey in 1086, the pattern of village settlement had been established in Breckland.

The Norman foundation of monasteries and abbeys resulted in much of the area being given to religious houses. Two of the wealthiest Benedictine monasteries in the country, Ely and Bury St Edmunds, owned much of Breckland between them. Ely held Lakenheath, including its rabbit warren, Brandon, Bridgham, Feltwell and Northwold. The Abbot of Bury owned the manors of Coney Weston, Culford, Elveden, two Fornhams, Herringswell and

Mildenhall with its prosperous fish market. The Archbishop of Canterbury, the Bishops of Rochester and Thetford and the French Bishops of Bayeux and Evreux all had manors in Breckland.

There were only a few religious houses in the area. Cluniac priories were founded at Thetford in 1104 and at Wangford before 1155; Thetford also had a Benedictine nunnery, a Dominican friary and houses of the Austin Friars and the Canons of the Holy Sepulchre. In 1170, an Augustinian priory was established at Ixworth. About 1220, Sir Hugh de Plais, Lord of the Manor of Weeting, gave land at Bromehill, to the north of Weeting Castle, to the Augustinians who established a priory there.

Lay lords who held land in Breckland included the Duke of Lancaster at Thetford and Methwold and the Duke of Norfolk at Hockham and Kennett. Castle Hill at Thetford is the largest mound in East Anglia. The Normans constructed it of chalk with a wooden pallisade on top, but no evidence of a stone keep on it has been found, so probably the site was abandoned when the castles at Norwich and Castle Acre were built. Weeting Castle was a fortified manor house. Built around 1180 by Ralph de Plais, it had an aisled hall with wings and a residential tower of three storeys. Some of the flint walls still stand to a height of 4 metres and the site is surrounded by a moat, now dry.

In the Middle Ages, especially when the climate was warmer, between 1100 and 1250, Breckland was extensively cultivated and marginal land brought into production. Close to each village were the 'in-fields', further away were the 'out-fields' and further still were the 'brecks', stretches of heathland broken up for cropping for a few years and then allowed to revert back to heathland.

Most large flocks of sheep were owned by the abbeys. In the twelfth century, there were 1,154 sheep in one flock at Elveden; 2,525 at Barnham and 3,000 at Lakenheath, with full-time shepherds.

In very cold weather, the sheep were confined in sheepcotes especially built on the edge of the pasture land. The Abbot of Bury paid for the sheepcote at Fornham St. Martin, while Lakenheath, with so many sheep, had three!

Over-cultivation and over-grazing on these Breckland sandy soils led eventually to their impoverishment. From the end of the thir-

Saxon Hut, West Stow Country Park

Ruins of Weeting Castle

teenth century onwards, there were extensive sand blows and village communities abandoned the marginal land. In Breckland, there are twenty-eight deserted villages whose populations dwindled over three or four generations. These include Kilverstone, Knettishall, Riddlesworth, Roudham, Timworth, Wordwell, Middle and West Harling. Often all that remains is a church which may be redundant or in ruins and a few scattered buildings. A deserted village, Godwick, near Swaffham can be explored and the hollow way of the mainstreet, the site of the manor house, water-mill, pond, villagers' houses and their garden plots traced clearly on the ground.

After the Dissolution of the Monasteries (smaller abbeys in 1536, larger in 1539), the monastic lands in Breckland were bought by local families, including the Bacons of Culford and the Kitsons of Hengrave Hall. The latter passed to the Gage family, after whom the greengage was named, as it was first grown at Hengrave. The practice of buying up manorial units meant that some villages that had previously belonged to different landlords, came under a single ownership for the first time. Most smallholders could not compete and moved away so that by the end of the seventeenth century Breckland was less populated than at any time since the Domesday Survey.

The population of New England, America, came to have links with Breckland in the seventeenth century. On 27 July, 1649, the Long Parliament passed an Act 'founding a corporation for the promoting and propagating of the Gospel of Jesus Christ in New England'. The New England Corporation raised £12,000 by public subscription and used it to buy property in London and also Eriswell Manor which it owned until 1869. The rents paid by the tenants were used to support missionary work in America. Some of the cottages in Eriswell have the initials NEC on them.

Faden's map of 1797 records the establishment of large estates, as the very rich landlords bought out their impoverished tenants. In 1785 Sylvanus Swan purchased 800 hectares around Riddlesworth; Mr. Wright reclaimed 800 hectares of heath at Kilverstone, marled the land for crop production and also farmed sheep on it. At West Tofts, now in the Stanford Battle Area, Sir Payne Gallwey turned heathland into a new landscaped park and made a plantation 14 kilometres long!

The first Enclosure Act in Breckland was for land at Hilborough, in 1768. During the Napoleonic wars, 1790-1815, there were forty-nine Enclosure Acts in the area. New farms were built on the former heaths and warrens, straight tracks and roads made to the enclosed fields and shelter belts of Scots Pine were planted for windbreaks.

The changes in agriculture together with the effects of the Napoleonic Wars, led to increases in prices for staple foods. The introduction of the Corn Laws in 1815 caused unrest and riots throughout East Anglia. In Brandon, on 16 May 1816, a crowd of about 200 gathered in the market place demanding 'cheap bread, a cheap loaf and provisions cheaper'. The crowd only dispersed after the Riot Act had been read.

By the beginning of the nineteenth century, 6 per cent of Breckland had been made into parks surounding large houses. These included Brandon Park, one-time home of Dorothy Paget; Shadwell Park, Wretham Park and Lynford Hall; Merton Hall, the estate of Lord Walsingham; Euston Hall, the home of the Duke of Grafton, and Elveden Hall.

By the 1850s the cheap imports of American grain made cereal growing in Breckland unprofitable and it was one of the first agricultural areas to become depressed. Much of the land went out of production and it was let for shooting. In 1912, on the Elveden Estate, it is recorded that 3,247 game were shot by five guns in a single day!

Some of the surplus agricultural labour found employment as navvies on the railways which, from 1845, were being constructed through Breckland. The first ran from Stratford north of London, to Ely and then on to Brandon where it linked up with the Brandon to Norwich line, also finished in 1845. In 1865, plans for the Thetford and Watton railway were put forward. Railway cottages were built of clay lump and stations of flint at Stow Bedon and Wretham. The line was opened on 26 January 1869 and the route was extended to Swaffham by 1875. It carried both passengers and freight and was especially busy during both World Wars as it served Barnham camp and Watton and other bases. It was closed in 1965. It was known as 'The Crab and Winkle' line and the disused track is part of the Great Eastern Pingo Trail.

Wherever you go in Breckland, there is an inescapable sense of the past. Walk along the Icknield Way at Cavenham and look out across the heath and you are looking at a landscape shaped by the people who lived and worked in it through the centuries. Beyond the pine trees are the settlements founded by the Romans and Saxons in the valley of the River Lark; cattle and sheep move across the land as they did in the Middle Ages and as the heath shimmers in the heat of a summer's afternoon, the feeling of past history is ever present.

A typical Breckland hedge

Chapter Three

FLINT

Wherever chalk occurs, there flint is also found. Flint is usually found in discontinuous seams when the pieces are termed nodular or in more or less continuous layers termed tabular. At Beer in Devon, where the chalk meets the sea in the form of cliffs, the layers of flint can be clearly seen. There is evidence that the flint which ended up on the beach after a cliff fall was used by Neolithic man for fashioning into tools and weapons, and from places such as this he probably realised that good quality flint could be mined from chalk elsewhere. The remains of ancient flint mines can be found in many places in the south-east, but the largest concentration by far is at Grimes Graves, a site a few miles north-east of Brandon in Suffolk, under the care of English Heritage.

During the sixteenth century records show that Grimes Graves was rented as a sheep walk. Its ancient origin had already been forgotten and superstition had already been built up about it. Consequently, its name, by which it is still known, bears no relevance to its true purpose. Grim was a chief god of the Saxons and the 'graves' part of the name is derived from the German 'graben' meaning pits or diggings, but the reason for the numerous hollows remained a source of curiosity and speculation for many centuries.

As a result of some very early excavations, it was thought to be the site of a fortified settlement occupied by the Iceni tribe before the Roman invasion. In 1868 Canon Greenwell started a systematic excavation of some of the hollows. After three years of arduous and sometimes hazardous digging, he was able to show that the workings were the infilled sites of Neolithic flint mines. This was the first time that the origin and the importance of the site had been realised.

24

Between 1972 and 1977, under the supervision of the British Museum, an extensive exploration of the site was undertaken with the aid of aerial photography. It is now known that the site extends over at least 36 hectares and contains at least 600 pit workings. More pits were opened and the contents of pottery, bones and other relics carefully sifted out from the infilling debris. It was estimated that about 8 tonnes of usable flints could have been taken from one of the pits examined.

The qualities needed in a stone or rock to be used for tool making are hardness, tenacity (breakability) and homogeneity. Hardness is essential for a tool which will be used for felling trees, cutting, scraping, killing animals and butchering their carcasses. Hardness is a disadvantage if the rock does not have a low tenacity, that is, it must break relatively easily when it is knocked with a 'hammer stone' and it must be homogenous so that it has a consistent and predictable mode of fracturing.

Flint has these properties and Neolithic man learned to make a very wide range of tools from this basic material. Presumably learning from centuries of previous experience, he perfected the art of working with flint. Somehow he discovered that the black floorstone flint of the Grimes Graves area was the best quality for tool making and was prepared to go to astonishing lengths to mine it.

Early exploitation of the site was probably limited to shallow working of the sloping ground, where the floorstone was near the surface and could be worked on an open-cast principle. But when this source was exhausted deeper mining techniques had to be employed.

The depth of a mine was determined by the position of the floorstone. Mines were as much as 10 metres deep with a diameter varying from 6 to 8 metres. The spoil of sand and chalk from a new pit was used to infill a worked-out shaft, hence the present day hills and hollows appearance of the site. The miners used red deer antlers for picks. The brow-tine was used as the pick and other smaller tines were removed. Vast quantities of discarded antlers have been found with 500 antlers recovered from a single shaft. The total number of antlers used during the long period when the site was in use (from about 3,000 to 2,000 BC) must have been astronomical but at the time the red deer was ubiquitous in the forests which then covered Breckland and antlers were readily available.

Having made the effort to sink a shaft down to the floorstone, miners then drove galleries into the hard chalk to extract as much of the flint as possible. These galleries were very extensive and some of them may have broken into a gallery of another shaft. The large pieces of flint had to be hoisted to the surface.

Flint responded well to the skilfully directed blows from a hammer stone to break off flakes. These could be further refined into daggers, scrapers, blades, arrow heads and a host of other tools to be used in the everyday life of their makers. Larger pieces had flakes worked off until only a core of flint remained. This was then fashioned into an axe head to be hafted on to a shaft. Axes were probably the single most important product, as they were needed to cut down trees and shrubs to clear land for growing crops . There was also a considerable demand elsewhere for the axes and they must have been valuable for bartering in exchange for other commodities.

Flint always fractures in a characteristic way. On each flake there is a striking platform on which the flaking blow has been made. Below this there is a bulb of percussion and to one side a much smaller bulbar scar. On a larger flake, very fine fissures run down the long axis, and waves or rings occur round the shorter axis.

Flakes showing these features can be found in many places throughout Breckland. The activity of Neolithic man must have been enormous and widespread. With the onset of the Bronze Age, about 2,000 BC there was a fairly rapid changeover from stone to metal tools and weapons. Grimes Graves is recognised as the oldest industrial archaeological site in the country. Perhaps it was also the site where workers were first made redundant!

The flints which the Romans used in their walls were probably picked up from the fields and were mainly used as rubble for infilling the cavities formed by the two outer walls. Flints used on the outer walls may have been roughly worked but there is no indication of real skills having survived from the Neolithic Age. The Romans knew the value of slaked lime in making the mortar for binding their walls and therefore may have had pits in the chalk and found some of the flint while extracting it.

There is another long break in the history of flint until the

Middle Ages, when it began to be used in ecclesiastical buildings and in many large secular buildings. The flushwork on many of them clearly demonstrates that a new age of flint knapping had arrived, but there is no reason to suppose that this had any particular association with Brandon or Breckland. There are numerous examples of very fine knapping of flint for building throughout the south-east and much of the material used must have been obtained and worked on or near to the building site. Roads were very primitive and the distance over which such heavy material was transported would have been kept as short as possible unless barges could be used.

Guns were first invented in the fourteenth century. They were fired by a smouldering piece of cord, which was touched on to the gunpowder and were called matchlock because of this. They were of limited use as the fire on the cord was easily extinguished by rain or windy weather. The only way that it could be relighted was with a strike-a-light, an operation which could take at least several minutes.

The principle of the strike-a-light was to strike the steel a glancing blow with a piece of flint. The harder flint knocked off small particles from the steel, which were white hot and if directed on to some very dry tinder would eventually start a smouldering fire which could be used to re-ignite the matchlock cord.

Strike-a-lights remained the main form of ignition until the invention of friction matches in the early years of the nineteenth century. A box, containing tinder and one or two steels and flints, sometimes had a candle holder on its lid. Sometimes the boxes were a very basic design but often they were very elaborate.

It is thought that the first flint-fired gun was invented in the early years of the seventeenth century. This introduced a mechanism which ensured that sparks thrown by a wheel from a flint held in metal jaws were directed on to the priming powder to fire the gun. The wheel lock gun was not very successful and it was expensive to manufacture because of its complicated mechanism.

During the Civil War, 1642-1651, the matchlock gun was as much used as any other weapon and this was the first conflict where guns were used on any considerable scale. In the second half of the seventeenth century a new flintlock firing mechanism was invented. The flint was still held in metal jaws but the priming powder was covered and kept dry by an L-shaped steel or frizzle. When fired, the flint was thrust forward on a strong spring. It hit the frizzle, forcing it forward and at the same time causing a shower of sparks to cascade on to the now exposed powder.

This became the standard method of firing guns for the next century until the percussion cap was patented in 1807. The new flintlock mechanism was a vast improvement on the old. It was much more reliable as the powder was kept dry and, providing a good flint was used, there were very few misfires. A musket known as Brown Bess was introduced into the British Army in the early 1700s and remained in service until after the Napoleonic Wars.

During this war, 3 million muskets alone were manufactured. Huge numbers of pistols, carbines, fowling pieces and other types of flintlock guns were also made, causing an almost insatiable demand for gun flint. Brandon flint makers became the main suppliers of the Army, and gun flints made from the dark floorstone flint were regarded as the best obtainable.

The emergence of the Brandon gun flint manufacturers as the most significant in this country, dated from 1790 when the Master General of the Board of Ordnance placed an order for 100,000 flints 'of the best sort at 20 shillings (100 pence) per 100'. This was a much higher price than that paid for flints from other sources and suggests that the workers in the area were already producing flints renowned for their quality.

The Master General's cousin, Charles Sloane (later Lord Cadogan) had acquired the Santon Downham estate in 1778. On the estate 'fine black flint' was found relatively near the surface in some places and was easy to dig out. Remains of flint pits have been found in the area. Even in those days it was perhaps a considerable advantage to have friends in high places for commercial gain.

In 1804 a further contract was placed for a monthly supply of over 370,000 flints from the Brandon knappers. In 1813, as the Napoleonic Wars approached their final phase, Brandon flint masters were supplying 1,000,000 gun flints per month, which provided work for about 160 knappers and flint miners!

A regular and reliable source of flint nodules was needed to ensure that deliveries could be maintained. Some flint nodules would have been obtained from chalk workings in the area. Pits which supplied chalk for use in mortar and whiting manufacture, produced a few tons of flint but this was inadequate to keep the gun flint industry going. It became necessary to mine the flint as a specific operation, especially as the prime need was for black flint.

Ling Heath, a few miles south-east of Brandon, became the main area for mining. This was a large area of barren heathland which had been allocated to Brandon parish when it was enclosed. A miner could have one mine being actively worked and another marked where his next shaft was to be dug. After the turf and vegetation had been removed, a shaft was dug through the overlying sand down to where the chalk began. It was extended in stages of about two metres and was just wide enough for the miner to move up and down. Each successive stage was at right angles to the last to allow the maximum penetration of daylight.

The shaft was extended until the floorstone was reached. The flint was then systematically mined by burrowing galleries into the chalk. Nodules of flint were broken out from the surrounding chalk and manhandled to the surface. Each was lifted a stage at a time while the miner climbed up with the help of toe holds cut into the chalk. Most miners worked alone. The only light was from a candle usually fixed into their caps. This also provided them with an estimate of the time which could be judged by the amount the candle had burned down.

At the surface, the flint was piled into heaps, known as jags, ready for carting into Brandon. A jag or cartload was sufficient for up to 18,000 gunflints, depending on the quality of the flint. Miners had to pay groundage on each load to the parish council. Much of the chalk raised in this way was made into whiting and the remaining debris was used to re-fill shafts when they were disused.

The first task of the knapper was to break the large nodules supplied by the miners into quarters of a convenient size to handle. This was done with a large hammer. At first any odd pieces of flint were removed and then it was broken down until each of the pieces had a smooth, even, 'striking' platform and could be rested on the knee for flaking.

While quartering and flaking, the knapper wore a leather pad on his knee. With his flaking hammer he worked systematically round the flint, striking off long flakes. The final process was to fashion the gun flints. For this a very light hammer and an anvil fixed to a block from a tree trunk were needed. Gun flints were struck from the flakes, and then sorted by eye into a variety of categories depending on their size.

Most knappers worked in small brick sheds, originally built for other purposes such as keeping livestock, storing implements and more general uses. These were poorly constructed and draughty and consequently, it became the common practice to block all holes with sacking to keep out the cold winds. The result was that the atmosphere in which the knappers worked was dusty with silica thrown off the flint by their ever-busy hammers. There was some respite during the summer when they could work outside whilst quartering and flaking, but most preferred to work at their blocks in their customary places when knapping.

The consequence of working so constantly in dusty conditions was that silica accumulated in their lungs to produce silicosis, from which many of them died early and few reached the age of fifty. Often, it seems that cause of death was recorded as pulmonary tuberculosis, due to incorrect diagnosis in the early years but now it is usually referred to as 'knappers rot'. In the later years of the industry the condition was much relieved by the use of masks, dust extractors and improved heating and ventilation.

After the heyday of the Napoleonic Wars and the victory at Waterloo in 1815, orders ceased and the industry plunged into deep depression. The final blow, as far as the Army orders were concerned, was its adoption in 1838 of the percussion cap cartridge which had been patented in 1807. Flint workers joined other distressed and unemployed workers in May 1816 in the riot in Brandon.

This was followed by a period of painful re-adjustment and was by no means the end of the industry in Brandon. Demands for Brandon gun flints continued to come from countries such as Turkey whose army used flintlock guns long after they had been discarded by the British. Other orders came from China and South America, but principally from South Africa, where flintlock guns were used until the mid-twentieth century. At present (1994) there are still knappers at work on a part-time basis fulfilling the needs of muzzle-loading gun clubs and the building industry, as building permission is only granted in some conservation areas if flint is used for exterior walls.

Some present day knappers are capable of producing replicas of Neolithic Age weapons and tools.

Mausoleum, Brandon Park

Chapter Four

BRECKLAND RABBITS

Rabbits are not native to this country but were introduced here by the Normans. There is no mention of rabbit warrens or coneys (the name by which rabbits were known until the eighteenth century) in the Domesday Survey of 1086, so it is thought that the first introductions were not made until the twelfth or early thirteenth century.

Rabbits were natives of warm areas of Europe and it took years for them to become acclimatised to the cold, damp and harsh climate of this country. At first, losses from diseases were very high but it was eventually discovered that they could be bred and reared successfully on land which was free-draining, particularly in areas of low rainfall. These conditions were ideally met in Breckland which was to become an important centre for commercial exploitation of rabbits though it was by no means confined to this area.

Even when rabbits escaped into the wild, the indigenous population which developed tended to thrive best on light soils where they could easily burrow and the vegetation could be grazed down to a very low level. Although they could be found virtually anywhere, they were never so numerous on the heavier soils into which they could only burrow with difficulty and there was a danger of waterlogging. Grass and other vegetation grew more consistently on these water-retentive soils but rabbits often got wet when grazing and probably a greater proportion died of disease due to the cold, damp conditions. About 99% of wild rabbits died in the mid 1950s as a result of myxomatosis. This had a dramatic effect on the economy of Breckland and is still causing changes to the vegetation and natural ecology of the area.

The word 'warren' first appeared in medieval documents and at that time referred to an open area where rabbits were kept. When first introduced, rabbits were kept in small numbers in open areas which were not enclosed. It seems that when the population was very low and food was plentiful, there was very little or no movement away. At this time the rabbits only provided food for their owner and his family, but as the commercial value of their fur and meat increased, large warrens enclosed by banks were established.

Place-names relating to rabbits occur frequently in Breckland and are evidence of the importance of rabbit-farming to the economy from about the fourteenth century until the occurrence of myxomatosis. Names such as Thetford Warren, Black Rabbit Warren, Warren Wood, Warren House and Coney Weston abound in the vicinity of Thetford and Brandon.

Medieval documents distinguished between 'free warren' and 'rabbit warren'. Free warren bestowed on the holder sole right to kill the beasts of the warren (an area of land) which could be taken by a large hawk i.e. pheasant, partridge, hare, and rabbit. By the end of the thirteenth century these rights had been granted for most of the East Anglian villages. Rabbit warren referred to land where rabbits were kept in a specified area.

The Prior and Convent of Ely were granted the right of free warren in Lakenheath in the mid-thirteenth century and at about that time established a rabbit warren there. This was maintained by the bishops and their private successors until the Second World War when most of the land was requisitioned by the Ministry of Defence for building Lakenheath aerodrome. Also in the mid-thirteenth century, the Bishop of Ely established Brandon Warren and other ecclesiastical houses joined in exploiting this rich source of food and revenue. The Abbot of Bury St Edmunds had Mildenhall Warren, the Bishop of Rochester, Freckenham Warren, and the Duchy of Lancaster had Methwold Warren.

By the mid-eighteenth century, boundary walls had become common. The walls prevented the valuable rabbits from straying and thus avoided a loss of income. Straying rabbits caused damage to crops and young trees and whilst keeping them in, the walls also helped to keep natural predators such as foxes, weasels and stoats, out. Within an enclosure the warrener was able to keep a better watch on his animals and poaching was made more difficult, although it remained a serious and constant threat to the stock.

The banks, normally built from sods of turf, were about 0.6 metres wide and nearly 18 metres high. There was usually some form of capping to deter animals from escaping should they get to the top of the wall. Furze, gorse, blackthorn, hawthorn, or a thick layer of reeds were among the materials used for this purpose. Some banks around Thetford Warren had an inside facing of stones to prevent burrowing. At Mildenhall Warren, where there was no such protection, rabbits did burrow through and to prevent large losses the warrener had to make regular inspections of the banks and fill up the holes.

F.W. Turner in 'Memories of a Gamekeeper - Elveden 1865-1903' describes how Lakenheath Warren was protected in the later years of the nineteenth century by 'a huge bank 4 feet 6 inches (1.35 metres) high, perpendicular on the inner side, flat on the top for a width of 2 feet 6 inches (0.75 metres), sloping outwards to 6 feet (1.8 metres) at the bottom'. On the top were placed gorse faggots. As this warren was crossed by the Brandon to Barton Mills road, long wing extensions to the bank were maintained along it to prevent the loss of rabbits. A number of men were employed during the summer to repair the banks and, at the same time, trapped vermin and predators.

When wire-netting was used on some warrens from the nineteenth century onwards, it had to be well-supported to deter rabbits from jumping over and also dug well into the ground to prevent them from burrowing under it.

Shortage of food was perhaps the main reason why the rabbits tried to escape. Sometimes crops were planted within the warren but unless they were well protected they had very little chance of growing beyond the seedling stage. Deep-rooted plants, such as sow thistle and dandelion, were favoured by warreners as they continued to grow throughout the summer except in the severest of droughts.

Sometimes, supplementary food had to be brought in; hay, turnips or swedes were especially grown for this purpose. In severe winters, when nothing else was available, gorse was cut from the open heathland and carted into the warrens. This was particularly useful when a snow cover limited normal grazing.

Severe sandstorms occurred in drought years where the rabbits had grazed down every scrap of vegetation so exposing the sandy soil to the wind. At Freckenham in 1550, the storms caused so much aggravation in the village that the inhabitants destroyed all the rabbits and their burrows. At Eriswell in 1809, the storms caused the loss of about 0.3 metres of topsoil, and on one occasion enough sand was blown from Lakenheath Warren to block the Little Ouse over 6 kilometres away.

A continuous war had to be waged against vermin and predators. Tunnel traps with spring-loaded doors, pit traps and gin traps were used against rats, polecats, weasels, stoats and foxes until flintlock, and later, percussion cap guns, became available. In the heyday of rabbit warrens many predatory birds such as hawks, eagles and red kites were common in Breckland. These were caught in pole traps (long since made illegal) which were round, spring-loaded gin traps. They were placed on the top of a pole or mound of earth and baited with dead rabbits. Great care was needed to ensure that the traps were set in places where they would not inadvertently catch the rabbits they were there to protect.

Poaching was another cause of concern for warreners. At first, poachers worked on their own, intent on catching rabbits only for their own consumption. Penalties for anyone caught poaching were very harsh in the eighteenth and nineteenth centuries. For stealing a rabbit a person could be transported for a number of years (really a life sentence as very few ever returned), whipped, fined or imprisoned. To evade arrest, poachers formed gangs to raid the warrens and vicious fights with warreners often took place.

Various means were employed to try to discourage poachers. Dry sticks were strewn over the main pathways so that footsteps could be heard from a distance. The spring-loaded gun was used to alert warreners and gamekeepers. This was triggered off by a trip wire strung across a pathway. When it fired, the poacher could be seriously injured and even if he was not hurt all the rabbits and game were frightened away and the warrener alerted.

Even within the confines of a warren, rabbits were still difficult to catch. Ferrets were used to flush them from their burrows into purse or long nets. Purse nets were small and fastened closely over the entrance to a burrow. To be fully effective every hole had to be covered, which was not easy, as the entrances to some were hidden by vegetation or scrub. The alternative often used was a net about 90 metres long staked out across the direction in which the rabbits were expected to run. Rabbits which ran into the net became inextricably entangled in the mesh, enabling the warrener to catch and kill them.

Whenever ferrets were used, they were muzzled to prevent them from killing rabbits in their holes. They were usually on a line so that their handlers could trace where they had stopped. This was usually when a number of rabbits had been scared into a blind alley from which there was no escape and the ferret remained near them.

Warreners, when using ferrets, always had a lurcher to catch any rabbits which bolted. The favourite dog was a cross between a greyhound and a collie because of the quick turn of speed inherited from the former and the hardiness and thick coat of the latter to withstand all weathers. This same cross was also the poacher's favourite dog.

Some warreners also used a tipe or tip-trap for catching rabbits at night. A pit, perhaps one metre square, and two or three metres deep, was dug into the sand or chalk. The sides needed reinforcing with stone or flint to keep them vertical on the sandy soils, but this was not necessary on chalk. The top was covered with a door hinged across the middle and bolted when the trap was not in use. To catch the rabbits, the top was covered with food and when they had become accustomed to feeding there for a few days, the bolts were unfastened and the rabbits fell into the pit. Dozens of rabbits could be caught in a single night in this way.

Some of the rabbits were eaten by the owners of the warrens but most were sold. An advertisement in the 'Ipswich Journal' in 1755 urged poachers to bring their rabbits to Newmarket three or four times each week in twelve-dozen lots, for eventual sale in London. Some of the rabbits were skinned before leaving the warrens as the skins were valuable and in great demand for clothing and trimming. The carcasses were salted before despatch. Until railways had been built barges were used to take some of them by river to Cambridge and King's Lynn, from where they could be sent further afield.

Warrens were in isolated parts of the countryside well away from villages. It was considered necessary to have lodges within the warren where a warrener and his family could live and work. These had to be substantial structures serving as fortresses against marauding gangs of poachers. Built normally of two storeys, on a high spot, they provided look-out points from where a watchful eye could be kept over the whole warren. On some of the bigger warrens there were two or more lodges.

The ruins of Thetford Warren Lodge can be seen to the south of the Thetford to Brandon road. Only the central tower remains after a fire in 1935 destroyed two wings and all the surrounding wooden buildings. The walls of flint and chalk mortar are 0.9 metres thick and the windows on the ground floor are very small. There is a narrow doorway with a hole above it for dropping missiles on intruders. A narrow stairway leads to the principal rooms on the first floor. The lodge is built on high ground, although this is not very obvious now that the warren has been afforested. In what was probably a courtyard there is a well about 30 metres deep. This was served with a crank and pulley, with one bucket coming up while the other went down.

The night's catch was brought to the lodge to be skinned and the skins stretched out on racks to dry. This warren of 1200 hectares was owned by the Prior of Thetford. In its heyday in the middle of the nineteenth century the yield was almost 30,000 carcasses per year.

Work at Lakenheath Warren was severely disrupted during the First World War but in the first few years after hostilities ceased, 81,000 rabbits were caught annually by shooting, ferreting, trapping and netting; later when rabbit numbers had recovered in two good years, 129,000 and 124,000 respectively were killed.

The commercial farming of rabbits declined during the nineteenth century when the wild population exploded and they became a major pest throughout the country. Farmers striving to produce crops in rabbit-infested areas fought a continuous battle against the pest. On some fields it became impossible to produce winter-sown corn because of the depredation caused by the constant grazing of rabbits during the winter when crop growth was slow. Spring-sown corn fared little better; although it grew faster and there was more hedgerow vegetation for the rabbits to feed on, it was harvested

Warren Lodge, Thetford. 'I found him as melancholy as a lodge in a warren'
from 'Much Ado About Nothing"

later and thus suffered more severely from the effects of summer drought.

Fencing to exclude rabbits was very expensive and the profitability of Breckland crops was too low to warrant the capital outlay. When in the 1920s and 1930s farming became very depressed, much land was abandoned to the rabbits. The only way to make any money was to catch them. Farmers could then earn enough to survive and pay the rent by selling their skins to factories in Brandon where they were processed ready for making into felt in factories in other parts of the country.

Farming began to recover in the late 1930s and on some estates rabbit-proof fencing was erected on an extensive scale. After the erection of the netting, the first operation was to exterminate rabbits from the enclosed land before cropping commenced. Regular maintenance of the fence was then needed to block any holes made under the netting and to repair broken posts.

At the outbreak of the Second World War the Army acquired land for tank manoeuvres and battle-training. Some of the land which had rabbit-proof netting was used and all the fencing destroyed. This became a prohibited area and no trapping was possible throughout the duration of the war. When the land was de-requisitioned, fences were re-erected and it is reputed that one order was for 80 kilometres of netting. In the first six years after the end of the war on one estate, 50,000 rabbits were killed annually but the rate had fallen to 20,000 by the time myxomatosis decimated the rabbit population in the mid-1950s. Although this disease killed a staggering 99% of the population with the remarkable fecundity of rabbits gradually numbers have increased to such an extent that in some areas they are having to be controlled by traditional methods in order to protect crops.

Rabbits in large numbers can be seen on parts of Cavenham Heath, a reserve managed by English Nature. The skin processing industry was an important part of the life of Brandon for at least 150 years. One firm, founded in 1790, was still functioning in the 1950s until myxomatosis became endemic. One factory employed 70 workers and the other 150, but they were forced to close through lack of skins.

Before the First World War, much of the work was carried out in cottage sheds where out-workers, mostly women, earned a little to supplement the reduced earnings of their husbands, who worked in the gun flint industry which was in decline. Women queued up on Friday evenings with their wheelbarrows, prams or whatever transport they could muster to receive skins to be worked on during the following week. These were handed out in 'turns' of 60 skins or 'tallys' of 120 skins. There was an almost insatiable demand for their labour as the two factories used up to 15,000 skins per day.

When the skins were received at the factory the first operation was to thread them on string and hang them up to dry. This was the monotonous work that school leavers up to the age of seventeen did every day except Friday, when the dry skins were taken down and allocated to the out-workers. Their job was to open out the skins and stretch them, and trim off the nose, legs and other odd pieces of fur. The trimmings were kept and eventually sold back to the factory, from where they were sold as a type of shoddy (a waste product of the wool industry) to Kentish hop growers. After trimming, the fur was then pulled using a pulling knife to remove the hair as rabbits have two distinct coats, one outer coat of coarse guard hairs unsuitable for felting and a soft furry undercoat.

On return to the factory, the skins were chemically treated so that the fur could be separated from the skin. The fur was packed into sacks and despatched to felt-hat manufacturers while the remnants of the skins were sent away for making glue. Nothing was wasted.

The fur had to go through several more processes before it had felted together sufficiently to be moulded into hard hats, bowlers and other felt products. The felt was processed using mercury. Men doing the work developed mercury poisoning, causing limb shake and contorted features; hence the expression 'mad as a hatter'.

The Brandon factories also handled skins from other animals including foxes, hares and stoats. One worker, born in 1916, has recalled the long hours worked between the two World Wars. At one time, the working day was from 6am to 5.30pm Monday to Friday and from 6am to 4.30pm on Saturday. Factory gates were closed at 6.02am and any worker locked out was deducted a quarter of a day's pay. Christmas Day was a holiday and on Boxing Day workers went beating for shooting parties. For this they received 5/- (25p), a bottle of beer, a piece of cheese and a chunk of bread. There was also an annual holiday when the factory owner hired a train to take workers and their families on a day excursion to Yarmouth.

Just before myxomatosis the factories were using 1 million skins from Australia, 1 million from New Zealand, 1 million from this country and 1 million hare skins each year.

Warren Lodge, Thetford. Detail of door

Warren Lodge, Thetford. Detail of defensive window

Chapter Five

THETFORD FOREST

Prior to the First World War much of Breckland was open heathland interspersed with arable farmland and woodland. On the heathland sheep competed with rabbits for every blade of grass and the arable farmer competed with the rabbits and summer droughts in producing crops of rye, barley and hay. The main areas of woodland had been planted during the nineteenth century to create, or enhance the value of, large shooting estates. There were also smaller woods which had been self-generated.

There was no tradition of managing woods for timber production. When the war broke out in 1914 and overseas supplies were cut off, Canadians were employed to oversee felling and the training of local labour.

It was no easy task to cut down trees with only axes and cross-cut saws. Apart from the hard work, skill was needed to get the trees to fall safely in the right direction. Branches then had to be trimmed off before the trunk could be pulled out by a team of horses. In some places, light railway tracks were put down to make this task easier. Trench warfare created an enormous demand for sawn timber and posts, and there was an increased need for home-produced pit props when they could no longer be imported.

Wartime shortages and the awareness that most of the suitable trees had been felled during the war, gave rise to concern for the future and demonstrated the need to formulate a forestry policy. To accomplish this, in 1919 the Government established the Forestry Commission. During the early years, the main activity centred around acquiring land for afforestation. In the 1920s and 1930s huge areas of trees were planted in many parts of the country and in 1922 a start was made in establishing Thetford Forest, which was to extend eventually to over 20,000 hectares and to become the largest lowland forest in this country.

After the boom years of the First World War, farming was plunged into depression by a rapid fall in prices during the 1920s. Breckland farming was very badly affected due to the marginal nature of the land. Rents had inflated during the war but within a few years the depressed prices made it impossible for occupiers to honour their commitments. Such was the poverty that many farmers only managed to carry on by virtue of catching rabbits to sell for meat and fur.

When tenanted farms became vacant, the owner had great difficulty in getting a new tenant and even if he succeeded, the rent obtained was abysmally low. Some farms were even let rent-free for a year or two rather than allowing them to remain empty as weeds and rabbits soon took over where land was not cultivated.

When the Forestry Commission was looking for land, it soon found willing sellers in Breckland and was therefore able to acquire a large area. This was gradually extended when more landowners offered to dispose of their land.

The Commission established its headquarters at Santon Downham which still remains the nerve centre for all activities. Over 300 houses were built to accommodate forestry workers and virtually created a new village. Other cottages were built within the forest to house workers who were needed on site to cope with the day-to-day management and emergencies such as forest fires. Their isolated dwellings are often occupied by people anxious to have a peaceful retreat remote from the stresses and strains of urban life.

Drought, searing winds and unseasonal frosts had to be taken into account in the selection of trees to plant. In the early years, the choice was influenced by trees already growing in the area as seed was collected from them. Gangs of workers went out in the autumn to collect cones from Scots pines, acorns from oaks and mast from beeches. A special machine was constructed at the Santon Downham centre to separate seeds from the fir cones and to prepare other seed for sowing.

As the forest expanded, demand for labour was such that camps were established at a number of centres. These were provided by the Ministry of Labour as instructional and training centres for the unskilled and unemployed men. The workers were required for the construction of roads, clearance of scrub, cleaning out ditches which had been neglected for many years and other tasks beyond the unaided resources of the Forestry Commission. Four permanent camps were built. The one at High Lodge was used for displaced persons after the Second World War, and recently became the centre of activities for some of the episodes of the TV series 'Dad's Army'. The camp has been demolished and High Lodge is now the focal point for the leisure activities of the Forest Enterprise part of the Forestry Commission.

Before any planting could commence, large blocks of land were surrounded by rabbit-proof netting. Intensive rabbit control measures were undertaken until the pest had been virtually exterminated from the area. Even so, deer, which gradually increased in numbers after the earlier plantings provided shelter and food, still did considerable damage to some young trees.

The seed was sown in nurseries located in various places scattered throughout the Forest. After two years, seedlings were lifted and lined out for a further two years until they were big enough to be planted out. At the peak of the planting programme, 80 hectares of nurseries produced seven million seedlings per year. This was enough for 1420 hectares when planted at 5000 per hectare. A single shallow furrow was ploughed out for each row. A man placing the seedlings in the bottom of the furrow, in a slit made with a spade, could plant at the rate of 1,500 per day.

These initial plantings were in blocks of 10 hectares separated from each other by wide rides for fire breaks and access. Scots and Corsican pines established well but Douglas fir and European larch were not so successful. Broad-leaved species and larch were planted along all the public roads and today are an important feature of the forest as they enhance the visual appeal of the road sides and are not part of the regular felling programme.

For the first few years after planting, weeds are kept under control. Those surrounding the seedling trees compete with them for moisture, nutrients and light, and if left smother most of them and even the survivors grow very slowly. After a few years, when the trees are well established, they begin to smother the weeds and eventually to shade the ground to such an extent that very few plants survive.

After 16 to 20 years, according to the growth that has been made, thinning or brashing starts. Of the 2,000 trees planted, about 1,500 survive until brashing begins. At first 2 in every 30 rows are taken out to give better access into the forest, making later thinning easier. The cleared land also provides space for stacking the usable poles.

Also at this stage, misshapen trees and any that are branched due to the centre having been grazed out by deer, can be removed. Successive thinnings at 4 to 6 year intervals remove more trees, until eventually only 150 remain to grow to maturity.

When the first thinnings were made, a depot was established near Brandon railway station, where they were processed and prepared for the various outlets. There were three main uses: the thinner poles were used for wall board and the thicker were selected either for pit props or for pulping at paper mills.

During the early 1960s the forest came into full production requiring 250 hectares to be clear felled each year. At this time the Brandon depot was handling about 125,000 cubic metres annually. The demand from the various markets fluctuated from year to year. In the 1970s, annual disposal in a typical year was 17,000 cubic metres for pit props, 42,000 cubic metres for saw mills and the remainder for paper pulp, hardboard, wood wool for packaging, fencing poles and a variety of other minor uses. Some of the twisted branches and other off-cuts regarded as waste was used for making into charcoal.

The Brandon depot was closed in 1988 due to a drop in demand for its products. Pit closures and the modernisation of mining methods introduced by the coal industry drastically reduced the amount of pit wood needed and without this market, the depot was no longer a viable enterprise. At the time of closure the depot was employing 38 workers.

A new era in the mechanisation of harvesting the trees started in 1991 with the introduction of the Grapple Harvester. This machine, costing at that time £135,000, is capable of felling, stripping off branches and sawing the trunks into pre-determined lengths. Its steel jaws are wrapped round the base of a tree, which is then felled

Grapple Harvester, High Lodge

Forwarder, High Lodge

46

with a circular saw blade. If it is worked for a 12 hour day it can fell about 250 trees per day. Forwarders, which are self-loading timber carriers, work alongside the harvester to transfer the trunks to a clearing from where they can be picked up by lorries.

Stumps are removed from the ground and bulldozed into rows where they are left to rot as is too expensive to remove them from the area. Any small trash is chopped with a flail machine and then the land is ready for replanting. Seedlings raised in finger fibre pots are planted by machine. The land is sprayed with a residual herbicide to protect the young trees. Repeat sprayings are carried out until the trees are able to smother the weeds. Sprays of fungicides and insecticides are carried out where they are considered to be necessary. Regular thinning of the stand is done in the traditional manner to remove surplus and misshapen trees but now hand saws and axes have been replaced with the staccato rhythm of a chain saw.

With the closure of the Brandon depot, a changed pattern of marketing became necessary. In the early years of the 1990s, thousands of tonnes of small round wood and the top sections of trees were exported to Scandinavia from east coast ports such as King's Lynn, Boston and Ipswich. This is used in the pulping mills and the ships carrying the timber over, often bring paper back on the return journey. In all, about one quarter of total production is exported. The bulk goes for sawn timber, as this gives a much higher return.

The October 1987 storm caused devastation in Thetford Chase and throughout the Forestry Commission's woodlands. In East Anglia it was estimated that 600,000 cubic metres were blown down. To help to avoid a massive dumping of trees on the market, it was decided to establish a wet log storage site near Lynford Hall. The technique had been pioneered in Denmark and Germany but this was the first trial in this country. The huge stack of logs was kept moist, which meant that they could be marketed slowly over a long period as market requirements dictated. The final logs were sold in December 1992 and even then the timber was still sound enough to meet customers' demands.

In the mid-nineteenth century, Sir Richard Sutton, the owner of Lynford Hall, planted an arboretum in the grounds. This is now under the control of the Forestry Commission and is open to the public. Among the oldest trees are very fine specimens of sequoias, some of which are over 130 years old and over 35 metres in height. After a period when little management work had been done, the arboretum was taken over by the Forestry Commission. Fallen and dead trees were removed and unwanted trees felled. A systematic planting scheme was commenced and now the arboretum contains an excellent selection of old mature trees and an equally good stock of younger trees to ensure its continued existence.

The forest abounds with wildlife but while many species do no harm to the trees, others can be very destructive. The forest can tolerate a certain number of harmful animals but if some species were allowed to go unchecked, it would be very difficult to establish new plantings and the continuity of the forest would be threatened.

In some parts of the forest, newly planted areas may need protection from rabbits by fencing. Although they are being vigorously controlled, rabbits are becoming less sensitive to the myxomatosis virus and unless checked the population could soon reach the pre-1950s level. Huge losses of young trees, caused by gnawing and stripping of the bark, would result.

Equally destructive are the grey squirrels which are now found throughout the forest, although they were not present in the early 1960s. In some years over 2,000 have been killed in an effort to prevent serious damage to young plantings. On the other hand, the red squirrel, which had the forest to itself before the grey squirrels became numerous, does not damage trees.

Chapter Six

THE NATURAL HISTORY OF BRECKLAND

When man first started to live in Breckland, the higher ground was mainly forest and the river valleys marshy land. Early settlements were near to rivers which gave access to the area. The rich deposits of flint were exploited for tool making, especially for axes with which to clear the forests so that the light and easily worked soils could be cultivated. Antlers from the large numbers of red deer which then roamed the forests provided raw material for picks, used by miners extracting flint from pits dug into the chalk. Eventually, the land was virtually all cleared and as a result of the combined effects of human activity, wild animals, climate and the soil, became largely open heathland until Enclosure started towards the end of the eighteenth century. Since then, man's activities have largely created the landscape of today.

The countryside in Breckland is now a combination of pine forests, pine shelter belts, arable farmland, heathland and river valleys. Of these, perhaps the most striking features are the rows of Scots pine, planted as Enclosure hedges to divide holdings and to help to reduce sand blows. In the latter half of the nineteenth century, shelter belts of pines and coverts were planted during a period when shooting interests were of more concern than farming for large estate owners. The trunks of the old twisted distorted trees with most of the lower branches missing, when glimpsed in the sunshine or silhouetted against a morning or evening sky, epitomise the spirit of Breckland. As soon as they appear on the horizon the traveller knows that this unique landscape is nearby.

English Nature recognises Breckland as nationally and internationally important for its dry heathlands and diverse wetlands and the wildlife which these habitats support. There are 42 Sites of

Special Scientific Interest (SSSI) occupying 8,360 hectares or 8.7% of the area, including four National Nature Reserves and about 600 hectares owned or managed by the Norfolk Naturalists Trust and the Suffolk Wildlife Trust. In the early 1990s endangered or rare species in Breckland included 34 flowering plants, 8 birds and 155 insects and other invertebrates.

The decline of heathland is the chief reason that wildlife is under threat. Because of changes in agriculture, forestry, myxomatosis, town and road developments, the area of true heathland has declined from 29,000 hectares in 1900 to less than 7,000 hectares in 1990. The problems are made worse by the fragmentation of what remains. Movement of wildlife from one small area to another is restricted by huge blocks of trees or intensively farmed land. Some of the areas are too small to provide suitable habitat for shy birds and animals. Much of the heathland which remains is under threat from invasion by shrubs and trees. Until the mid 1950s large numbers of rabbits grazed the heath so tightly that seedlings of almost any plant had great difficulty in surviving. Although the rabbits are increasing, they are not numerous enough everywhere to prevent the further spread of pine and birch, both of which have seeds which are easily spread by the wind. Since 1945 on Lakenheath Warren pines have spread to cover 50% of the area.

Much of this heathland has been irretrievably lost for it will eventually become woodland as the task of removing self-set trees and shrubs from all the area is far beyond the resources available. However, determined efforts are being made to restore the balance on some of the worst affected areas. At Barnham Cross Common, a local nature reserve, a conservation group was formed and carefully selected sites cleared of intrusive vegetation. As soon as it was removed, stitchwort, meadow saxifrage and speedwell reappeared. It is hoped that by a combination of volunteer workers and rabbits, the aggressive vegetation can be controlled and typical Breckland heathland flora restored.

On Thetford Heath, a national nature reserve, a different approach has been taken. After myxomatosis, gorse, broom and Scots pine began to invade and threaten the natural flora. Most of these plants have been cleared and the area has been fenced so that it can be grazed by sheep. This is because the existing population of

Knettishall Heath

Cavenham Heath, late summer

rabbits is not high enough to improve the sward by grazing the rougher vegetation. The combined effect of rabbits and sheep will, it is hoped, restore the heath flora and provide suitable nesting conditions for stone curlew and wheatear.

There has also been a marked increase in bracken on the heaths due to changes in management and lack of grazing. In the nineteenth century bracken, used as litter, for roofing, covering root clamps and for firing, was extensively harvested in Breckland, mainly by smallholders who possessed commoners' rights over large areas of heathland. This practice persisted until the beginning of the twentieth century. There was a show of strength by the commoners at Lakenheath as they thought they were in danger of losing their rights when a gamekeeper objected to bracken being cut. On one day, 55 men with scythes arrived to cut bracken, the traditional starting day being 29th August, St John's Day. Typically, a villager would cut an acre per week for 14 weeks to provide litter for cattle-yards over the winter period. In the last 100 years some was cut with a sail reaper, an implement which was a fore-runner of the self binder; it left the bracken in small untied sheaves. On some reserves cutting is being undertaken to help to control bracken but in some areas herbicides are also being used.

The open land of Breckland is often dominated by heather and ling. This is where the soil is acid and only a relatively few plants are able to tolerate the lack of lime. Much of Cavenham Heath is covered with heather or bracken but there are also some fine birch trees growing there. There is also birch woodland both on the dry sandy soil and wet area near the River Lark.

A different habitat can also be seen on the Cavenham Reserve. This is where a high proportion of rabbits has remained and the turf is very short. Here the stag's horn lichen thrives and this area is a remnant of what much of Breckland was like at the beginning of the twentieth century.

Where the soil contains chalk, there is a type of grassland rich in flora not unlike that found on the traditional downland pastures. Here bird's foot trefoil, thyme, common rock rose, quaking grass, eye-bright and many other plants can be found. The area surrounding Grimes Graves is a particularly good example of this type of open land. In the spring it is a profusion of colour dominated by rock roses and thyme. There are also common spotted, pyramidal and twayblade orchids. In 1993 a single plant of the splendid pink appeared which was a first record for this reserve.

Along verges of roads, footpaths and bridleways, the showy blue viper's bugloss is often present. It is probably the most noticeable of all the Breckland flowers because of its distinctive colour and upright habit. Other plants in this category include mullien, dyers greenweed, soapwort and musk mallow.

Heathland is ideal territory for snakes. Both grass snakes and adders are quite common. The only indication that a snake is near-by might be a rustle in the undergrowth. On sunny warm days one may be seen basking in the sun. A snake gliding through the water of a mere is not an uncommon sight.

MAMMALS

A wide range of mammals are present throughout Breckland but are seldom seen because so many are mainly nocturnal and also they hide in the long vegetation where they live.

Grey squirrels are the most commonly seen of all the mammals and in picnic areas where they are fed they become very tame. They were introduced into this country from North America at various times between 1876 and 1929 and were so successful that they have colonised most of the woodlands in England although they were not seen in Thetford Forest until 1968.

During the eighteenth century red squirrels were so numerous throughout the country that tens of thousands were killed as pests. From 1900 to 1920 there was a rapid drop in population and they disappeared entirely in some areas. Since then the decline has continued. One of their last strongholds in southern England was in Thetford Forest but only a few remain and they are the subject of intensive study under the Species Recovery Programme. Possible reasons for the decline of the red squirrel include competition from the larger grey squirrel, disease and the lack of suitable habitat.

The decline is not thought to be entirely due to grey squirrels because of the differing habitat requirements of the two species. While grey squirrels are mainly found in deciduous woodland and

Grimes Graves in June

parkland where their omnivorous feeding habits are satisfied by a
wide range of foodstuffs, the red squirrel seems to prefer conifer
plantations where their more specific need for seeds and nuts can
be satisfied. In Thetford Forest, in the early years of planting, the
main species used was Scots pine but when it was realised that
Corsican pine had a better timber production potential, more
emphasis was placed on planting it.

Mature Scots pines produce a good annual crop of cones and provide a regular supply of food for red squirrels. Corsican pines have
less cones and not such a regular crop and are less able to sustain a
static population. To try to encourage them, mature Scots pines are
being left for the benefit of the red squirrels as they should then
have an assured food supply and tall trees in which to live.

Efforts are being made to feed the red squirrels but not to encourage the greys. Food hoppers have been designed with a long run
containing a weight-loaded trapdoor which, when the heavier grey
goes along, is activated allowing it to fall out while a lighter red
squirrel can proceed to the food. There is some difficulty in per-
suading the reds to seek food while the greys are well known for

Red Squirrel

their ingenuity in overcoming obstacles to reach it.

As a further part of the programme, red squirrels are being bred in captivity and later released back into the forest. Survival and behaviour of these squirrels is being monitored by radio tracking and field observations. In the study area the grey squirrel population is being controlled by the use of cage traps.

Red, roe, fallow and muntjac deer are all present in Breckland but are mainly confined to the forest during the day. The larger species can be seen in early morning and late evening, grazing on fields and crops growing near the woodland. In 1990 there were about 150 red,

150 roe and 4,000 fallow deer in the forest. The red deer are descendants of introduced East European wild stock and are larger than those which are found in Scotland.

Hoof marks are a good guide to the whereabouts of elusive deer. Sometimes they clearly show where a track is used regularly and where they may be seen by a very patient observer or a lucky walker. On good days in the forest, fallow, muntjac, roe and red deer may all be seen within an hour or two but it is much more usual not to see a single animal during a three or four hour walk.

Deer safaries are included in the events organised by Forest Enterprise. These take place in the evening and with the invaluable assistance of a forest ranger, several will be spotted. Even then, they can be difficult to pick out by the untrained eye, especially when a deer is lying down and its well-camouflaged head is just about the same height as the vegetation.

Deer numbers have to be controlled by culling carried out by forest rangers. A browsing deer will eat the shoot of a young tree, causing it to be stag headed (without the main stem) and useless for timber. It is not until a tree is about ten years old that it is reasonably safe from browsing and the effect of deer rubbing their antlers against the bark exposing it to attack by disease and insects. Annually, 400 to 500 deer are culled with 270 rifles in the hands of rangers and licence holders and it is thus carried out as humanely as possible. The beasts to be culled are selected to keep the herds well balanced in terms of male and female and as healthy as possible.

Bats occur throughout Breckland and are encouraged within the forest by the provision of bat boxes. These are placed on tree trunks, often near to picnic sites. They resemble the more familiar bird nestboxes but lack the access hole which they have. The bats can enter through a very narrow space at the bottom of the boxes which they use only during the summer months. Some old tunnels near to High Lodge have been developed to provide suitable conditions for hibernation. The entrance has a grill allowing access for the bats but not other animals, and it is sealed off from human intruders. Only scientists studying the bats enter this sanctuary and their visits are limited and carefully monitored as their body warmth could cause a rise in temperature which would unsettle the bats if their stay in the tunnel is prolonged.

Goshawk on look -out post

BIRDS

One of the first records of birds in Breckland is in a document dated 1310 in which the Prior of Ely reserves for himself all the bitterns found on his marshes and fisheries at Lakenheath. There are no bitterns resident around Lakenheath now and no suitable territory for them, yet Breckland still has several different habitats and a wide variety of bird species. These habitats include the rivers that cross the area, the meres, the agricultural land, Thetford Forest and the heathland, some of which is in nature reserves.

The Rivers Lark, Little Ouse, Thet and Wissey are breeding sites for mute swans, mallard, gadwall, tufted duck, coot, moorhen and kingfisher. Snipe and yellow wagtail frequent their banks with common sandpiper appearing on migration.

Langmere, Ringmere and Fowlmere, when full of water. support breeding populations of gadwall, tufted duck, teal, pochard, great-crested and little grebe, coot and moorhen. Garganey have bred on Langmere while Fowlmere with its areas of mud, is also used by waders, especially redshank, ringed plover and common sandpiper.

The fluctuations in water levels of these three meres - from empty to full - means that bird-watching there is rather unpredictable.

Thompson Water, at the south-west end of Thompson Common, is an artificial lake made in 1847 from a small tributary of the Wissey. It attracts many species, including waders, black terns and osprey on migration. In winter, there are Bewick's and whooper swans, teal, pintail, gadwall and goosander, wigeon and the occasional smew. In summer, reed and sedge warblers nest in the reed beds and great-crested grebe, little grebe, mallard, pochard and shoveler breed.

The meadows on the Thompson Common Reserve, grazed by a herd of Shetland ponies (owned by the Norfolk Naturalists Trust) provide nesting sites for lapwing, redshank and snipe. The wet woodland habitat of Stow Bedon Covert and Thompson Carr is ideal for woodcock, nightingale, redstart, sparrowhawk, willow and wood warbler and chiffchaff. Long-eared owls, great spotted and green woodpeckers can be seen on the Pingo Trail.

One Breckland farm of 3,640 hectares is renowned as an example of what can be achieved when conservation is considered alongside intensive agriculture. In 1993, 38 pairs of lapwing nested on 809 hectares where the land was drilled late, for carrots and parsnips. When the tractor drivers found a nest, they used a spade to lift it away from the path of their implement on to the land which had just been worked and the bird readily accepted the new site of its nest. Set-aside land left as bare ploughed soil provided nest sites for 8 pairs of ringed plover and 3 pairs of oystercatchers, while 6 metre wide headland strips, left unsprayed, are ideal habitat for skylark and grey and red-legged partridge.

The shelter belts of pine trees on the farm harbour crossbills and the areas of woodland planted by the Victorians as cover for game birds, support blackcap, hawfinch, garden and willow warblers and woodpeckers. A diversity of trees and berry-bearing shrubs attracts fieldfares and redwings in the winter months and large flocks of finches including bramblings feed on the rough ground. Eleven pairs of stone curlew also nested in 1993, proof that wildlife will respond to the creation of suitable conditions.

On East Wretham Heath there are areas of mature, deciduous woodland, mostly of beech and hornbeam and pine trees two hundred years old. Hawfinches nest in the hornbeams and in 1975, 190 were counted there on one evening in mid-February. The list of species on the Reserve is quite impressive and includes barn, little, long-eared and tawny owls; green, great, and lesser spotted woodpeckers; blue, coal, great, long-tailed, marsh and willow tits; blackcap, chiffchaff, lesser whitethroat and whitethroat; garden, grasshopper, reed, sedge and willow warblers; goldcrest, spotted flycatcher; tree and meadow pipit; skylark; pied and yellow wagtail; crossbill; wheatear and woodcock. Passage and wintering birds of prey include rough-legged buzzard, hen harrier, short-eared owl and the occasional merlin and peregrine.

Weeting and Cavenham Heaths are perhaps the best places to see stone curlew, the bird which most seems to epitomise Breckland. With its pale buff and brown plumage it merges into the heath on which it nests. It has huge, yellow eyes for nocturnal vision, as it feeds by night on earthworms and beetles. In the 1940s about 1000 pairs were recorded in Breckland, but these had fallen to just 120 pairs in 1968. Breckland still has the largest concentration of stone curlews in the country. In 1993, 92 pairs reared 64 young. They return to their traditional breeding sites year after year; some, nesting on what are now ploughed fields, which retain their flinty, sandy, heath-like appearance, have their nests noted by farmers so that agricultural machinery can avoid them.

Weeting Heath supports several pairs and is an excellent place to see larger flocks as they gather there before migration. It is specifically managed for these birds, with grazing rabbits maintaining the short turf that they need. In the long summer nights, the high-pitched calls of the stone curlews carry across the heath, as beautiful and haunting as Breckland is itself.

Unfortunately, the continued presence of the stone curlew has not been matched by that of the red-backed shrike. Britain is on the northern edge of its breeding range so it has always been vulnerable to changes of climate which affect the availability of its insect food. In the country as a whole, there were 250 pairs in 1960, 100 pairs in 1970, 25 pairs in 1980 and only 2 pairs in 1987. The latter were in Breckland, near Santon Downham and were continually wardened by the RSPB during their nesting period. Sadly, in 1988 only one pair returned and in 1989 there was but a single bird

Stone Curlew

Nightjar

recorded, so for the first time in living memory no shrikes nested in Breckland.

Thetford Forest is the largest commercial pine forest in lowland Britain and the Forestry Commission works assiduously to create and maintain a variety of habitats for wildlife within it.

In the pines, crossbills nest and small artificial ponds have been dug to provide water for them. Brambling and siskin feed on the pine cones in the early spring, as the warm sun opens the cones to reveal the seed inside. Blue and coal tits, turtle doves, goldcrests and even firecrests also live in the conifers. There are 2000 hectares of broad-leaved woodland, alder and willow carr, oak and sweet chestnut shelter belts and roadside plantings of beech, larch and oak, all of which provide vibrant colour in the autumn. Hawfinches nest in such trees, especially near Santon Downham and there are also nuthatches, warblers, coal, long-tailed and willow tits.

In the 1960s, the Forestry Commission began a pattern of clear felling about 300 hectares a year which has proved particularly beneficial to some bird species. The forest now consists of 10 to 15

Crossbill

61

per cent of such clear felled areas, with conditions akin to those of heathland, encouraging wheatear, whinchat, stonechat, meadow pipit, red-legged partridge, woodlark and nightjar.

Breckland's woodlark have increased from 40 pairs in the late 1970s to 145 singing males in 1992, which is 20 per cent of the British population. On mornings in April and May, the woodlark sings for up to half an hour while flying in circles high up in the sky.

When the clear felled areas are colonised by brambles, dogrose, elder and nettles, and the newly planted seedling trees are 1 to 2 metres high, they are ideal for song-birds such as tree pipits. yellowhammers and whitethroat, while grasshopper warblers also nest in the ground cover, especially along the banks of earth and trash constructed by the foresters. In the dense scrub are golden pheasants of which Thetford Forest has the largest self-supporting population in Britain. Where the pines have been thinned for the first time, after 25 years growth, hobby, sparrowhawk, kestrel, jay, magpie, tawny and long-eared owls nest and there are blackcap, chiffchaff, and willow warbler. Dead tree trunks are left to provide nesting sites for great spotted woodpecker, tits and redstart and as perching posts for birds of prey.

There were only 6 recorded goshawks in Norfolk between 1929 and 1967, one being at Lynford Arboretum, but in 1993 near Mayday Farm, at least one pair was known to have bred successfully and there were possibly another 5 or 6 breeding pairs.

It is probably the nightjar which has responded most rewardingly to the creation of habitats suitable for it. A Forestry Commission funded RSPB project investigating the breeding requirements of woodlark and nightjar, has found that new plantations are used by nightjars for up to 15 years and that a mixture of bracken for nesting and young trees for song and display posts are ideal. Newly felled plantations and areas up to five years after replanting, hold the biggest nightjar numbers which increased from about 170 pairs in 1981 to 230 pairs in 1989 representing 10 per cent of the British population.

Nightjars are faithful to their nest sites when they return from Africa in mid-May. The birds incubate their eggs during the day and feed at night on moths and other insects. It is an unforgettable experience to be in the forest as the day ends in the long, warm, still twilight of summer and suddenly in the dusk, the soft, floating glides of the nightjar are just discernible. Sometimes, the male claps his wings as he displays, but most evocative is the sustained liquid churring song repeated over and over again as night falls over the forest and heaths of Breckland.

Entrance to bats' tunnel

Chapter Seven

BRECKLAND CHURCHES

Breckland churches are not perhaps as well-known as the wool churches which dominate much of Norfolk and Suffolk but they have their own attraction, charm and treasures. This chapter looks at some aspects of these churches and in more detail at Santon Downham, Lakenheath and East Harling as they are especially rewarding both architecturally and historically.

Some churches are in lovely settings. Beachamwell St Mary stands on the edge of the village green. Great Cressingham St Michael is on rising ground so that its tower is seen to best advantage. Hockwold St Peter is encircled by tall trees and is adjacent to the Tudor red-brick hall. Weeting St Mary is near the moated site of the ruined, fortified manor house.

Some churches are now in ruins as a result of village decay or desertion. St Andrew at Little Cressingham has its tower and west end in ruins. All Saints, on the edge of Knettishall Heath, St Andrew at Roudham, St John and All Saints at Beachamwell and St Margaret at Hilborough are marked only by fragments of their walls. St Lawrence at the north end of Eriswell village is scarcely recognisable as a church since it was converted for use as a dove-cote in the seventeenth century though it retains two Decorated windows.

Flint was used extensively as a building material from the Saxon period to the Victorian restorations of the nineteenth century. It appears in Saxon round towers, in the walls of naves and aisles, and in the flushwork panelling of the thirteenth and fourteenth centuries. As late as 1879, Henry Clutton built the church of Our Lady of Consolation, on the Lynford Estate, of knapped flint. Brick came

Carved bench end, Lakenheath St Mary

Thirteenth century font, Lakenheath St Mary

into more general use in the fourteenth century and was used especially for clerestories, where the roof height of the nave was raised and in porches.

Thatching is the roofing material for both the nave and chancel at Beachamwell church and at All Saints, Icklingham where even the porch is thatched.

Saxon round towers are a feature of several Breckland churches including Merton, Weeting, Kilverstone and Breckles where the tower has a fifteenth century octagonal top with flint chequer-work panels and a succession of small, blocked circular sound holes. Beachamwell St Mary also has a round tower with an octagonal top of the same date, and very characteristic Saxon light-openings. Those on the south and east have two-lights divided by a baluster above which is a horizontal slab, while those on the north and west have triangular heads. Saxon long and short work can be seen in the north-west corner of the nave.

Gooderstone has a Norman tower of about 1200 into which has been inserted a Decorated west window. The staircase turret also remains. Thompson's rather isolated church has an unbuttressed tower of the fourteenth century, with a flushwork base and flint-panelled battlements.

There are excellent Perpendicular west towers at Great Cressingham and Hilborough, of similar design. The two churches are only about three miles apart and may have been the work of the same masons. At Great Cressingham there is a west doorway with a frieze of shields and crowned 'Ms' for St Michael; these also appear on the porch. Hilborough's tower is of knapped flint; its doorway has figures of huntsmen in the spandrels and above it a frieze of circles and shields and then a three-light window; the battlements are also adorned with shields.

Mildenhall's tower is 36 metres high and dates from about 1420. Until 1831, it had the addition of a wooden lantern spire. In 1864, the tower was replaced and the turret added. Wilton St James, now the parish church of both Hockwold and Wilton, has the distinction of a stone spire, one of the very few in Norfolk. Brandon's church has two octagonal turrets surmounted by pinnacles arising from each corner of the east wall of the chancel, giving it rather a continental appearance.

Porches are important as they are the first part of the church to be entered; they formerly offered shelter and were used for weddings, baptisms, funerals and penances as well as for trading and legal transactions. All Saints, Bridgham has flushwork panelling in the north porch and inside, the ceiling of the porch has a tunnel vault with transverse arches. The porch at Gooderstone has very unusual circular side windows, each with three trefoils within the circle. Rushford, once the church of the college founded there by Edmund Gonville (of Gonville and Caius College, Cambridge) in 1342, has a Perpendicular porch of knapped flint and brick with flushwork embellishment.

The north porch at Mildenhall dates from 1420 and is one of the largest in Suffolk. It has an upper or parvis chamber now used as a chapel. The ceiling of the lower porch is vaulted with much damaged carved bosses. Above the doorway are carved the arms of Edward the Confessor and St Edmund (Mildenhall belonged to the Abbot of Bury). The south porch, of similar date, has only one storey but the ogee-arched surrounds to the doorway are richly carved. The porch at Thompson has a massive doorway with three mouldings of decorative ironwork, dating from the fourteenth century and a key 40 centimetres long.

In their interiors, Breckland churches have features from the late tenth century onwards. Most were not rebuilt entirely in the Perpendicular style, probably because the local economy was suffering a decline at the time.

The Saxon period is represented by the massive arch at Beachamwell which joins the round tower to the nave. The tower arch at Breckles is early eleventh century and has a snake-band pattern on it. Brettenham retains a Norman doorway with patterned shafts, volute capitals and a zigzag motif around the arch.

The Early English style can be seen at Eriswell St Peter, in the wall arches of Great Cressingham's chancel, dating from 1300, and in the three stepped lancets at Gooderstone. At Mildenhall the chancel dates from 1220 but the east window was inserted in the early 1300s. The vestry was built at the same time as the chancel and has a stone vaulted ceiling and the narrow lancet windows so distinctive of this period.

Examples of Decorated architecture include the chancel at Thompson with its five-light east and three-light north and south windows, partially blocked. The chancel windows at Bridgham have reticulated tracery. At Weeting the window tracery is quite complicated, the east window being described by Pevsner as 'reticulated tracery broken at the top by an octofoiled circle'. There is a very beautiful doorway in Beachamwell church which led from the chancel into the former vestry. It has the ogee curves typical of the Decorated period and rich foliage.

There are some especially fine piscina and sedilia in Thompson church where they have broad low ogee-curved arches with green men among the carved leaves and trailing stems. At Hilborough the double piscina has cinquefoiled pointed arches and at Gooderstone the double piscina has trefoiled pointed arches.

The most interesting fonts (beside those at Lakenheath and East Harling) are those at Breckles, Bridgham, Hepworth, Merton and Thompson. Breckles is Norman on five pillars, one being in the centre and all having characteristic Norman capitals. The sides have blank arcading and rows of figures, including one praying and one with outstretched arms. Bridgham has two fonts; one is also Norman and came from the ruined Roudham St Andrew; the other is fifteenth century and has the scene of the Assumption carved on it, together with angels holding emblems of the Trinity with four lions resting against the stem. Hepworth St Peter was rebuilt after a fire in 1878 but the font cover was rescued. Its lower part is like a tiny castle, complete with battlements, towers and doorways at which soldiers stand guard. Merton's hexagonal font is fifteenth century and is carved with shields; against the underside of the bowl are angels whose wings delicately reach up and frame the shields. It has a crane for raising and lowering the cover. The font at Thompson is fourteenth century, octagonal, with traceried panels and a fifteenth century crocketted cover.

Medieval stained glass is rather uncommon in Breckland but Great Cressingham has a fifteenth century window depicting angels, bishops and kings. Merton has some pieces of medieval glass and there are fragments in the upper parts of the windows on the north and south sides of Mildenhall's chancel. At Gooderstone, in the east window of the south aisle, figures depicted in stained glass lean at all angles in order to fit the tracery.

Benches were virtually unknown before the fourteenth century as the congregation stood or knelt. East Anglian bench ends are renowned for the craftmanship, originality and the beauty of their carving, not only on the poppy-heads (from the French 'poupee', a doll, or the latin 'puppis' a poop) but also on the arm rests and along the traceried backs. Many Breckland churches have these exceptional benches. Gooderstone has a complete set of fifteenth century poppy-head benches with pierced, traceried backs and mythical beasts on the arm rests. Hilborough's benches are very similar but the arm rests have sadly lost their figures. Barningham has fifteenth century benches with arm rests which include a camel and an owl. In the nave at Wilton church there are bench ends showing a shepherd and his flock and the figure of Mercy giving help to prisoners. At Merton, the priest's seat in the chancel has carvings of a parson at his desk and a cellarer with a hammer and three barrels. Thompson has seventeenth century benches which are exceptional as they are in untreated oak and have a very lovely silvery-grey appearance. The two benches nearest the screen are dated 1632 and 1635.

Wooden pulpits began to appear in the fifteenth century and by the end of the seventeenth were sometimes two or three-decker, following emphasis on preaching laid down by James I. Merton has a two-decker pulpit and reader's desk while Thompson has a three-decker combining clerk's seat, lectern and pulpit with a tester sounding-board overhead.

Beautiful rood screens are a special delight of East Anglian churches. They separate the nave and chancel and hold images of the crucified Christ, the Virgin Mary and St John. Originally, the screens were brightly coloured and gilded, the lower dado adorned with the painted figures of saints and the traceried panels above holding the rood loft. They are represented in Breckland by those at Merton, Thompson, Gooderstone and East Harling. The screen at Merton is fourteenth century and is pierced by cusped tracery wheels. At Thompson, it dates back to 1330 and the base of another screen separates the south chapel, founded by Sir Thomas de

Shardelow in 1450, from the nave. At Gooderstone it is particularly lovely: the panels have paintings of the twelve apostles with angels around their heads and sections of the Creed around their bodies. At the extreme north end, for example, is St Peter holding the keys of heaven, with his portion of the Creed 'I believe in God the Father'. Along the top of the screen are brackets either for use as pickets for candles or for statues.

As in many East Anglian churches, the interior roofs are often so spectacular that they almost take one's breath away. Norman roofs were quite plain structures filled in by a truss or framework of timbers supported on oak tie-beams. The more elaborate, open form of roofing was developed in the thirteenth century and reached its zenith in the Perpendicular period, with waggon and hammer-beam roofs. The latter are typical of East Anglia; the hammer-beams are sometimes alternated with arched braces and adorned with figures, painted and gilded. Great Cressingham has such a roof. Hockwold has alternating tie-and-hammer-beams from which eight carved figures look down. Hilborough's angels in the nave roof have their heads damaged but those in the chancel are intact and carry symbols of the Passion.

Mildenhall St Mary is justly famous for the splendour of its roof, not only in the nave but also in the aisles. In the north aisle, six angels project out horizontally from the hammer-beams but, very sadly, their wings have been removed. In the six spandrels are some wonderful carvings including devils playing an organ, St George and the Dragon, Christ being baptised, the Visitation of the Shepherds and a hunting scene. Carvings on the braces reflect the wildlife of the area, with a dog barking at a boar and a heron eating an eel.

In the south aisle, the roof is decorated with carvings of swans and antelopes, the emblems of King Henry V. In the arched braces, a bearded figure is attacked by a wyvern (a creature with dragon's wings and eagle's feet) and a woman is holding a serpent's tail and two wyverns by their necks.

Other notable interior features of Breckland churches include the mechanism of the 1670 clock at the west end of the nave at Gooderstone and the seventeenth century brazier at Hilborough, used to heat the building. There is an hourglass stand fixed to the chancel screen at Merton, perhaps for timing sermons! The original consecration crosses can be seen on the walls of Thompson's church and wall paintings of angels in the fourteenth century chancel at Wretham. At Hockwold St Peter, the bells hang on an early fourteenth century frame, one of the few remaining in the country.

At Thompson are three parish chests for storing registers and documents. The Mildenhall chest of about 1300 is nearly three metres long, iron-bound and with the customary three locks, the keys being held by the vicar and two churchwardens to ensure that it could not be opened unless all three persons were present. Icklingham All Saints chest of 1360, carved in wrought-iron foliage, is now in St James in the same village. There is a cast-iron chest at Beachamwell designed by John Motteux and made in 1835 by Joseph Bramah of the firm of London locksmiths. Also here on a column at the south-west end of the nave, is a carved list of the quantities and prices of materials supplied to masons in 1340 surmounted by a strange head scratched into the stonework, known as the Beachamwell Devil.

Beachamwell has two brasses of vicars on the chancel floor, one un-named and the other of John Grymeston but both have their hands clasped in prayer and are wearing their priestly robes. Merton has a brass of William de Grey who died in 1495. He is depicted in armour with his five sons and five daughters. At Great Cressingham are brasses to Richard Rysle, 1497 and his wife; to Judge William Eyre, 1509; John Abarfield, 1518 and Elizabeth Jenny, 1538. West Harling church which now stands isolated and surrounded by fields, has a brass to William Berdewell and his wife, of 1490.

Monuments and memorials give very personal glimpses of the people who worshipped in the churches. Breckles has a memorial in the chancel to Ursula Hewyt who died in 1658. The inscription in Latin 'Stat ut vixit erecta ' means that she was buried in an upright position. In the tower is a tablet to John Stubing who was buried 'in the middle of this steeple' at the age of 107. At the east end of Beachamwell church is a memorial to John Motteux (designer of the chest mentioned earlier), lord of the manor in the nineteenth

Flint-work on the porch, East Harling, St Peter and St Paul

Lady chapel screen, East Harling, St Peter and St. Paul

century. This was erected by Charles Spencer Cooper, a close friend. The two met when involved in an accident in Piccadilly and Cooper helped Motteux. In gratitude Motteux bequeathed to him all his Norfolk estates, including Sandringham which was bought by Queen Victoria in 1861. East Wretham's churchyard has the grave of Sir John Deverance, an inventor and engineer who took out one hundred patents for his inventions.

Breckland churches also have links with national events and figures. During the Peasants' Revolt of 1381, John of Lakenheath, Chief Justice Cavendish and the Prior of Bury Abbey were all killed near Lakenheath by the rebels. At Great Cressingham, the Rector, Edward Franklin was slain by Roundheads in the garden of the manor house during the Civil War. The Nelson family held the living of Hilborough in the eighteenth century. Nelson's grandfather, father, brother and uncle were all rectors there; his aunt is buried in the churchyard as are two of his brothers who died before he was born. Nelson took the title of 'Baron Nelson of the Nile and Hilborough'. At Merton, the lychgate was erected in memory of the Reverend George Crabbe, grandson of the Suffolk poet. His friend, Edward Fitzgerald, the translator of the Omar Kyam, died in the rectory while staying with him.

Having looked at the features of Breckland churches, three are now examined in detail. The church at Santon Downham stands in a clearing, on the edge of the village green. It is built of rubble with stone facings, flint and brick. The external roofs of the nave and chancel are oak, replacing the former pantiles. A church is recorded here in Domesday (1086) but it was probably of wood. The western half of the nave is Norman with two typical doorways and two round arched windows, though from the outside the latter have been converted to pointed lancets. Above the south doorway is a carved panel showing an animal, perhaps a lion, with a trailing vine from its mouth.

The tower, built between 1460 and 1500, unusually with no buttresses, has names inscribed in the stone and flint-work around its base. They refer to villagers who bequeathed money in their wills to the church, all dating from 1463 to 1504.

Inside, the church has a peaceful, untroubled atmosphere. The chancel and the eastern half of the nave are thirteenth century. The font is contemporary, octagonal with a moulded stem and seventeenth century cover. The rood screen appears to have been altered at various dates but the painting of the lower panels may be original fourteenth century work. The south window of the chancel has some medieval glass but most of the stained glass is Victorian.

In the nave are tablets to the Cadogan family. Colonel the Honourable Henry Cadogan fought in the Duke of Wellington's army in the Peninsular War and was killed at the Battle of Vittoria in 1813. Lady Powlett, widow of the Lord Powlett whose hatchment is in the tower, planted the avenue of limes from the Thetford road to the village.

The church of St Mary at Lakenheath is full of delight because it contains so much of architectural and historical value. It stands on a slight rise in the middle of the village, in a large, walled churchyard. The exterior is an amazing mixture of building materials. On the south side is carstone, flint and Woolpit brick; on the north, there is some very attractive flint-work and a line of bricks which show where the roof level was raised; there is some septaria in the chancel. The tower, of the late thirteenth century, has a limestone base, flint chequer-work and some carstone; it is surmounted by a lead spire. On its western side a parvis was added in the seventeenth century to serve as a school room. At the corner of the south aisle, to the west of the porch, on the fourth stone up, is a very simple scratch dial.

There are Early English lancet windows in the chancel and Decorated windows in the tower and the north aisle. In the east-facing wall of the north aisle is an unusual window; it is circular but has a quatrefoil shape in stone tracery within it. In the north wall of the chancel is a small blocked doorway, a lancet window and traces of two arches.

When you enter the church, your attention is immediately caught by the wonderful Norman chancel arch but there is a great deal more to look at. The nearest pillar to the right of the font has the remains of a medieval painting showing St Edmund with his crown and a halo; he is holding the three arrows with which he was killed by the Danes. The pillars are fifteenth century but stand on thirteenth century bases which, in turn, stand on Norman shafts.

The thirteenth century font is exceptionally beautiful and may have come from Eriswell St Peter. It has a circular base, a central stem surrounded by eight shafts and flowers and foliage carved around the bowl. There are three ornamental brasses in the floor and eighteen matracies, mostly to the cloth workers of the parish. In the north aisle is a tablet commemorating Lord Kitchener, Secretary of State for War from 1914 to 1916 but remembered here as President of the London Society of East Anglians. The first Kitchener came to Lakenheath from Hampshire in 1666 to work as a bailiff.

It is perhaps the beauty of the carving in wood on the roof and benches, which is Lakenheath's greatest attraction. The pitched roof of 1460 has sixty angels among the tie-beams which are arch braced with queen posts. Among the larger angels with outspread wings are smaller angels. There are two figures positioned on either side of the chancel arch. The one on the left has a horrible face with protruding teeth while the one on the right has a serene, benign face. They represent evil and good.

The nave is filled with wonderful benches fixed to a continuous curb so that they appear to be on a platform, perhaps to contain rushes which may have been strewn on the floor. All the benches have pierced traceried backs and the carving of the poppy heads and arm rests is enchanting. There is an elephant, a lion, a beaver, a unicorn, acrobats, including one in a very contorted position, a hare, fish, priests reading books and either a tiger looking at itself in a mirror or a dog licking out a pan! At the back are wooden panels, possibly from a rood screen.

The church of St Peter and St Paul at East Harling is not only a very beautiful building but is also imbued with an atmosphere of times past and a sense of worship through the centuries. This church is a wonderful example of the Perpendicular style, almost untouched since about 1450. There are some vestiges of the earlier building dating back to 1300, including the lower part of the tower arch and belfry window, the base of the south wall, the lady chapel screen, the Herling tomb, the narrow west window and the doorway in the south wall of the chancel.

The nave with its tall graceful pillars is of a breath-taking height, lit by the eighteen windows of the clerestory. The font, decorated with quatrefoils and now with a seventeenth century wood cover, was probably from the earlier church. Across the west end of the nave is the lower part of a medieval screen with panels showing flowers and trailing foliage, and heraldic symbols such as crowns and unicorns.

At the east end of the nave is the pulley by which the pyx containing the consecrated bread was raised in front of the rood. Below is the base of the rood screen still richly painted with its medieval red, gold and green. In the chancel are six miserere stalls, four with their original seats and carved arm rests of a man, a lion, an eagle, a unicorn, a pelican with her young, a warrior about to strike with his sword and shield, and a dragon with a long tongue and twisting tail.

The east window of the chancel, given by Sir Robert Wingfield in 1480, is exactly as it was then, but it has not always been in place. During the Protectorate of Cromwell, the glass was taken out and hidden in the attic of the manor house; it was put back in 1736 when the Lovells sold the manor to Thomas Wright. It was removed again for safety in the Second World War and only replaced in 1947. The window depicts scenes from the life of Christ and in the lower part is the figure of Sir Robert Wingfield kneeling on a blue cushion wearing armour and a tabard of red, gold and black.

The lady chapel, at the east end of the south aisle, has an incredibly lovely parclose screen with a fan canopy, tracery ornamented with roses and heraldic devices, and owls, dragons. squirrels (eating nuts) and figures in the spandrels or on the panels. The bench fronts are richly decorated with ogee arches.

The wonderful roof reflects the skill of the carpenters. It is steeply pitched, rising to a height of 15 metres. The hammer-beams are richly carved and even the aisle roofs are adorned with angels.

East Harling is especially rich in its tombs which are very evocative memorials to the people who worshipped here. The oldest is that of Sir Robert Herling who served as a soldier to Henry V and died in 1435. He rebuilt the lady chapel so it is fitting that his tomb is there. It has an elaborately carved canopy with ogee arches and two figures holding shields. The carving includes unicorns, the fleur de lys, an eagle, and a pelican. Sir Robert's feet rest on a lion but his arms have been damaged as has the figure of his wife, Joan the heiress of the Gonvilles of Rushford. Sir Robert's daughter Anne has her tomb in the chancel with that of her first husband, Sir William Chamberlain. She died in 1502 and he in 1462. The brasses have been removed but the tomb is decorated with shields and has heraldic symbols on the vaulted arch of five canopies. Sir William and Lady Anne were the benefactors of the 1450 rebuilding. When he died, Anne married twice more, her third husband being Sir Robert Wingfield who gave money for the east window.

Also in the lady chapel is the characteristically Elizabethan tomb of Sir Thomas Lovell and his wife, Alice, who died in 1604 and 1602 respectively. Sir Thomas was Chancellor of the Exchequer to both Henry VII and Henry VIII. The tomb is in alabaster with a canopy, shields and pinnacles, all richly coloured. Sir Thomas is depicted with his sword at his side: his head rests on his helmet and his feet on the Lovell crest, a bundle of peacock feathers. Dame Alice wears a robe and ruff, an embroidered cushion is at her head and her father's crest at her feet. Other Lovell tombs are on either side of the east window in the chancel.

Other Breckland churches may seem rather modest by comparison with these three but each is worthy of a visit. Each has its own special atmosphere created by those who lived and worshipped there in the past and by those who worship there now and lovingly care for these buildings.

Angel Roof, Lakenheath St Mary

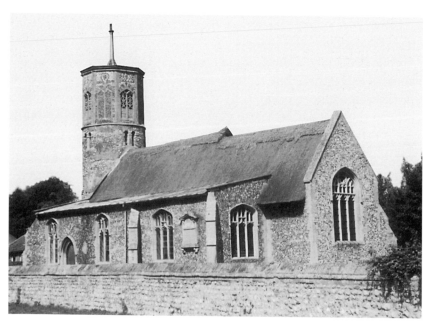

Beachamwell St Mary

Chapter 8

AGRICULTURE

The inherent low fertility and poor water-retaining capacity of Breckland soils combined with a very low rainfall, present farmers with considerable problems and challenges. In the Middle Ages, a system of farming based on sheep was developed. They roamed over the almost barren heaths by day and were brought back to the homestead at night. There they were confined to a relatively small area and their droppings accumulated until the land was fertile enough to grow a few crops, before it was allowed to revert to rough grazing again.

The Norfolk breed of sheep was popular until the agricultural improvers began to realise its deficiencies and started to cross breed it to increase the value of its wool and meat. Coke of Norfolk said of the sheep that 'their backs were as narrow as the rabbits' which shared the heaths with them but it was also acknowledged that the native breed could live in Breckland where nine-tenths of the other breeds in the kingdom would starve. It had long legs which were ideal for wandering over large areas in search of food from the scant vegetation and it was wild by nature. In spite of this it was relatively easy to fold at night.

Arthur Young (1813) wrote of the quality of the mutton, 'it being admitted at Smithfield, that as long as cool weather lasts, it has, for the table of the curious, no superior in texture or grain, flavour, quality and colour of gravy, with fat enough for such tables' and that the wool was 'fine being in price, per pound, the third sort in England.' An old rhyme in praise of the sheep runs:

> Old Norfolks will serve well enough
> To dung our sand - unless until

They prove that some outlandish breed
Are hardier and can further ramble
To pick scant fodder nimbler scramble
With strong bare legs and bellies high
Through brakes, broom, furze, heath wet or dry.

By the end of the eighteenth century, attempts were being made to improve the breed by crossing with other breeds. Eventually the Suffolk breed developed from crossing Southdown rams with Norfolk ewes. The new breed inherited the black face of the old and also a disease which is still a problem. This is scrapie, which was described by Vancouver (1794) with such accuracy that there is no doubt about its identity. He mentioned the change in the colour of the wool, the shedding of the fleece, the irritation which induced sheep to scratch against posts and hurdles and the unsteady gait as if in a fit. The common remedy was then, as now, the slaughter of animals showing symptoms of the condition.

The enclosure of land which began in the late eighteenth century, and the ever increasing demand for food from expanding industrial towns, gave new impetus to arable farming. Improvements could be carried out on land which was being farmed for the benefit of the occupier rather than the commoners.

The free-draining Breckland soils become acidic when chalk is leached down the soil profile and by the same process nutrients are also lost. In addition they contain a large proportion of fine particles of sand which are vulnerable to being carried in the wind in the form of dust storms. Because of this marling was widely practised.

In many parts of Breckland there is at least one marl pit in every field, evidence of the energy and effort that was put into improving the land by marling it. Remains of marl pits are also often encountered in the forests as they were not filled in when the trees were planted.

Marling was an ancient practice known to the Romans and there is little doubt that it was carried out on a limited scale in Breckland at least from the Middle Ages. There is a Lampit Hill which was shown on a map of 1338 as Lampythowe, obviously derived from loam pit. A clay pit was shown between Croxton and Thetford in 1509.

Marl was the name given to rather variable material, the nature of which depended on where it was dug. To be of benefit to Breckland soils, the marl had to be a heavy textured, calcareous clay which would give greater resistance to blowing, add nutrients and neutralise the acidity when it was spread over the surface. It was an expensive operation, with long-term benefits, and thus it only became a common practice when land was held on a long-term tenure. The process involved digging marl from a pit and then carting it to be spread evenly over the land.

Since all the work had to be done by hand-labour using horses and carts, it was essential to limit the distance over which the marl had to be carted. The pits were not very large, but deep, and are now commonly seen as conspicuous clumps of trees or shrubs within a field.

The amount applied varied considerably, depending on the farmer's conception of what was needed at the time and for how long he wanted the benefits to last. Some value from very heavy dressings would last for a hundred years. Some farmers preferred to apply small quantities more frequently. A reasonably average dressing was 50 to 60 loads, of 35 cwts each, per acre (approximately equivalent to 250 tonnes per hectare). When looking at remains of pits it is difficult to imagine how the carts were hauled from the bottom. One farmer devised a method using a capstan and a horse on the field, to assist getting the carts out but it is not known how universally this was used. In some of the larger pits it appears there was a track which gradually spiralled to the top round the edge of the pit.

The value of marling has long been recognised:

> He who marls sand
> buys the land
> He who marls moss
> shows no loss
> He who marls clay
> throws all away.

Having gone to the expense of marling, the land was cropped as much as possible, roughly following a Norfolk four-course rotation except that wheat was not grown. A rotation at the beginning of the nineteenth century might have been turnips, followed by barley, two years in ley, rye, turnips and so on. The turnips would have been fed to sheep folded on them and to cattle kept in yards during the winter to tread straw into farmyard manure, to help to maintain the level of organic matter in the soil. The leys provided grazing during the summer and hay for the winter.

But however good the husbandry, making a living from farming in Breckland during the nineteenth century was, to say the least, precarious. Many dry years were disastrous for all the crops and there was the constant problem of hordes of rabbits which must have ruined large areas. For the farmers there was the compensation that the rabbits could be caught and sold to help to pay the rent.

In the middle of the century, when imports of cheap grain undermined home production, many farmers could not make a living and land remained uncultivated and reverted to heath, unless it was planted with trees and shelter belts for game. Shooting became very fashionable at this time and large game estates were established in the area, and on these, crop and animal production became of secondary importance.

At the beginning of the twentieth century there was a brief revival because of food shortages during the First World War and the high prices which were obtainable. But the revival was short-lived and in the 1920s farming was again so depressed that land fell out of cultivation and the sale of rabbits was again often necessary to pay the rent. It was at this time that the Forestry Commission acquired the bulk of the land which is now afforested.

A new crop, sugar beet, was introduced into arable farming in East Anglia during the 1920s and 1930s. This became possible following the opening of processing factories at King's Lynn, Wissington and Ely. These factories could receive deliveries from barges, using the Rivers Wissey, Great and Little Ouse and Lark. Sugar beet was grown on contract and although the drought-prone soils of Breckland were not ideal for the crop, there was a guaranteed market and price for it. To some extent it could overcome lack of moisture in the topsoil by penetrating down into the sub-soil with its deep rooting system.

Asparagus was introduced by Captain Kidner in the 1920s in the Lakenheath area. It grew very well on the free-draining, sandy soils because of its deep roots and some years later Lord Fisher planted a considerable area on his Kilverstone estate. Since the end of the Second World War there has been a revival and expansion of the crop and Breckland is now one of the main growing areas in this country. One of Captain Kidner's varieties was used in hybridising a new variety called Royal Pedigree, named because it was grown at the former home of Lily Langtry, who was Edward VII's mistress.

Between the two World Wars, on the Elveden estate, there was a gradual reduction in arable crops and an increase in grassland and livestock farming. In the early 1900s the estate of approximately 12,000 hectares consisted of about 4,250 hectares of rabbit warrens, 1000 hectares of woodland and 3,500 hectares of farmed land, of which a little over half was arable. In the late 1920s, the second Earl of Iveagh began to pioneer changes to improve the agricultural output of the estate. During a three year period from 1927 to 1930, over fifty kilometres of rabbit- proof netting were erected. This was costly in labour and materials, as at the base the net was dug into the ground to prevent rabbits burrowing underneath it. After an area had been enclosed, warreners exterminated the rabbits before cropping commenced.

Dairy cattle were introduced on to two of the farms and large fields were sown with lucerne and cocksfoot. Where necessary, lime was applied before the lucerne was sown, as it will not grow in acid soils. This is another deep-rooted crop which can withstand all but the most severe droughts. Used either on its own or in combination with cocksfoot, it provided the Elveden cows with grazing for much of the year and with hay during the winter. At first all the lucerne hay was made on tripods. Whilst this could produce very high quality fodder, the method was very labour-intensive and eventually greater emphasis was put on making silage, especially as the herd size increased and as manpower became restricted during the Second World War. When it was decided to abandon milk production on the estate in the early 1980s, there were over 2,000 cows in the herds.

During the Second World War much of the heathland was reclaimed for crop production. A massive programme of liming was necessary as the calcareous constituents of the soil had been leached from the heaths, some of which had never been recorded as having been cultivated. Despite wartime shortages, enough tractors with deep-digging ploughs to bury the bracken and heather were available to undertake the work. Some of the soils were so impoverished of nutrients and trace elements that yields were very low, but detailed soil analysis and extensive experimentation eventually led to an understanding of the deficiencies which were causing the problems and how they could be corrected.

In the mid 1950s, myxomatosis swept through Breckland. This disease originated in South America and reached this country from France. It was so virulent that within a few weeks of reaching an area virtually all the rabbits were dead. The effect on farming was dramatic, even on farms where warreners had previously been employed to control the rabbit population. It became possible to grow crops on land where rabbits would have destroyed them before myxomatosis appeared and yields of some crops, such as cereals, were dramatically increased. There was still a food shortage and farmers were encouraged to reclaim more of the heathland, most of which is still cultivated, although not cropped every year due to the policy of 'set aside' and grants available in the ESA (Environmentally Sensitive Area) scheme.

In the late 1980s the Ministry of Agriculture, Fisheries and Food (MAFF) recognised that 'In Breckland the local soils and climate, together with the farmers' use of land, have produced a range of features which are unique to Britain. The heathland and dry grassland support a rich variety of flowers, birds and other wildlife and the cultivated land contains rare arable weeds'. For these reasons Breckland was designated as an ESA.

This is a voluntary scheme and 'farmers are invited to enter into agreements with MAFF which involve adopting or maintaining practices that will help to conserve or enhance the area.' These practices include the following: encouraging farming of heathland and dry grassland in the traditional manner so benefiting the indigenous plants and birds especially the stone curlew; leaving headlands unplanted to allow common arable weeds to grow (such headlands often produce a profusion of colourful flowers during the spring and summer) and maintaining the traditional hedges, ponds, ditches and other characteristic Breckland features. Many other provisions attract payment from the scheme to try and achieve a profitable and sustainable farming system in the area while, at the same time, protecting its unique landscape.

Perhaps the most important innovation in farming in the last forty years has been the introduction of irrigation. In many parts of Breckland it is possible to see huge pivotal or linear irrigation systems at work during the summer. Water may be obtained from deep boreholes sunk into the underlying chalk, or from reservoirs filled from rivers and streams during the winter. When a regular supply of water is available the range of crops which can be grown can be expanded to include vegetables.

The sandy soils, although they are sometimes very stony, are easy to cultivate and are accessible to farm machinery within a few hours or a day or two after heavy rain. They therefore lend themselves to phased drilling of crops, which is essential for a continuous supply of fresh vegetables to be achieved to fulfil contracts to supermarkets to which most of the produce is sold.

Carrots are widely grown. Normally the carrot grower hires land on an annual basis for his crop. He then does all the work involved from drilling time to harvesting. Early crops, often sown in January, are given protection with polythene. At first glance, these sheets look like an expanse of water, until it is realised that they sometimes occur on hilly fields. Even birds are deceived and many a duck or swan has had a startled landing on a polythene sheet. The covering provides a 'mini-greenhouse' effect and ensures that the crop is ready for lifting in May to start the season.

A continuous programme of sowing at regular intervals, using a number of varieties with different maturing dates, is maintained during the summer. If the land is dry, irrigation is used to encourage germination and growth. In the autumn, crops not required for immediate lifting are covered with straw or earth to protect them from frost. These crops are lifted in the spring and in most seasons will last until the early crops are ready for harvesting.

Carrot growing is now completely mechanised, with herbicides used for weed control, and pesticides for control of carrot root fly, aphids and any other pests which might be a nuisance in some seasons. The aim is to produce roots of uniform size, blemish free, which will wash easily for packing into pre-packs, or perhaps for selling loose.

The carrot grower has to have an enormous investment in machines to produce and harvest the crop and also to wash and grade it. There are, therefore, relatively few growers in Breckland, although the output is enormous. One firm which grows parsnips and lettuce as well as carrots, has its own fleet of articulated lorries carrying its logo, and employs between 900 and 1,000 to keep the farm and packhouse going.

Rye was one of the first crops to be grown in the area as it will thrive on poor, acidic soils where most other crops fail. Usually it is winter sown and ripens in June and July before all the moisture has disappeared from the light, sandy soils. It is the most conspicuous of the cereals as it has an ear with long awns and long straw.

Winter sown barley is also grown extensively as it also ripens early and thus avoids the most damaging effects of summer droughts. Wheat is grown on some of the better soils with a good water-retaining capacity.

Other crops which can be found in Breckland include linseed, with its very pale blue hue, oilseed rape with its eye-catching acid-yellow flowers, evening primrose with tall stems and pale-golden flowers and borage which at first glance appears to be a field of viper's bugloss.

Banks of wooden sheds, housing intensive poultry production, occur on many farms. These may be for table poultry, turkeys or egg production. As the area has a low human population density, these sheds are built in relative isolation from houses. The manure produced is welcomed by arable farmers to add organic matter and fertility to their land, but some is now used for the production of electricity in a generator commissioned during 1993 at Eye in Suffolk.

Traditional duck farming has not yet disappeared. Young duck-lings, penned on clean land, thrive on the dry soil where diseases are minimised by a continuous programme of moving them on to fresh land.

Light free-draining soils were for many decades used for outdoor pig keeping. The system became less popular when better profits could be obtained from using the land for arable cropping and indoor pig keeping became more fashionable. Now the trend is back to outdoor systems and once again arks and kennels are much in evidence. Broadly, there are two systems currently being followed. The most widespread is for breeding sows, usually housed in arks with semi-circular corrugated iron roofs with the weaners taken in doors for fattening. Sometimes the weaners are confined to kennels with runs where they are fattened in the open. These are moved regularly on to clean land to reduce the need for medication and to eliminate the need for cleaning out, while at the same time leaving droppings evenly distributed across the field.

Although Breckland soils are ideally suited to sheep, their numbers are relatively low on the mainly arable farms. Flocks can be kept for much of the year on the remaining heaths and rough grazings and then folded on to arable by-products such as sugar beet tops, to fatten in the autumn.

Shetland Ponies, Thompson Common

Chapter Nine

MILITARY ACTIVITIES IN BRECKLAND

On the map of Breckland between Watton, Mundford, Brandon and
Thetford there are numerous references to 'Danger Area'. Printed
in red, they are eye-catching and clearly delineate the area of the
Stanford Field Training Centre. This is known as the Battle Area
and is referred to as such in this book. This Battle area is in constant use by the armed services and access is therefore extremely
restricted, even to permit holders and organised parties.

There has been military activity in Breckland since the beginning of this century. Before the First World War, parts of the
heaths were used for infantry training. In 1911 the East Anglian
Manoeuvres involved up to 30,000 soldiers accomodated in a forest
of white bell tents on Thetford Warren together with their mules
and weaponry. As there were no made-up roads at that time,
columns of approaching troops were indicated by the clouds of dust
which they created as they arrived by road or from the railway station.

East Road, Thetford became a landing ground for military aircraft and for the first time the possibility of using aircraft to support infantry was tested. Shortly after the start of the First World
War, aircraft from Thetford and Feltwell used targets in
Lakenheath Warren for practice. Aircraft were unreliable by modern standards, and when in difficulty would land on any level piece
of ground including suitable roads.

Breckland was also used for tank practice and in 1916 a demon-
stration was arranged for Lloyd George. A military presence was
maintained between the two World Wars and aerodromes established at Feltwell, Watton and Mildenhall. After the start of hostilities in 1939 others followed including Bodney, East Wretham,

Knettishall and Tuddenham, all of which are now derelict, and Lakenheath which is still in use.

Also during the Second World War, dummy aerodromes or K sites were established at Eriswell, Low Warren and Cavenham Heath. Replica aircraft, made from wood and canvas and painted in full combat colours by RAF personnel, were dispersed to resemble an operational station when seen from the air.

Blenheim bombers stationed at RAF Watton in the early years of the war suffered very heavy losses. It was taken over by the American Eighth Air Force in 1943 when both Liberators and Flying Fortresses were stationed there. Secret agents were flown out in A 26 Invaders to be dropped in Germany and France. Some of the men who were parachuted behind enemy lines were never heard of again but many got back after making contact with British agents and delivering vital messages. Perhaps the record for a quick return went to an agent who reappeared in the mess at Watton four days after having been dropped in enemy territory!

In 1944, lengthening of the runways at RAF Lakenheath necessitated diversion of the Mildenhall to Brandon Road. After this the runways were used by heavy bombers of the USAF which still occupies the aerodrome.

Throughout the 1980s, F-111s, nicknamed Aardvarks because of their long noses, were flown from Lakenheath. These slender swing-winged aircraft were a familiar sight in the skies of Breckland. Aircraft from the base were involved in the American raid on Libya on 16 April 1986 and because of the long flight avoiding France, were refuelled in the air by tankers from Mildenhall. They were also used in Operation Desert Storm during the Gulf War of 1990-91 where they flew over 800 sorties.

By the end of 1992 all the F-111s had been replaced by the F-15 Eagle. This aircraft is a distinctive twin-tailed jet capable of flying more than two-and-a-half times the speed of sound. Although relatively quiet when in flight, the tranquillity of Breckland in the vicinity of Lakenheath is shattered by the ferocious roar when it takes off and lands. There is a good viewing area specially provided for 'plane spotters to the north of the base near Wangford church.

Mildenhall is also an American base where huge transport aircraft, converted tankers, AWACs and a wide variety of other types can be seen.

In 1940, land was required for army training and about 4800 hectares were obtained near Thetford, under Defence Regulations. This area was only available to the army for manoeuvering and not for firing live ammunition. In 1942, there was an urgent need to establish an area which could be used for integrated training of troops and air power, using live ammunition. It was decided that about 7,000 hectares in the Stanford area should be acquired for this purpose. This meant that the villages of West Tofts, Buckenham Tofts, Tottington, Langford, Sturston and Stanford had to be cleared and 600 inhabitants moved out.

Public meetings were held to explain the position and everyone was given three weeks to leave the area. Such was the patriotic fervour at the time, that the generals were applauded after they had addressed the meetings. People living in rented houses were promised that they would not have increased rents as a result of the move. This promise was kept but it proved impossible to allow residents to return after the end of the war, as was also promised. This was because of the danger of unexploded ordnance and the continuing need for a battle area for troop training.

The land was acquired by the Ministry of Defence by compulsory purchase in 1950. In 1990 it was expanded to nearly 11,000 hectares by a further purchase of land towards the north of the area.

By the 1990s it had become one of the busiest army-training areas in the country with training activities on most days of the year and an annual through-put of up to 85,000 troops, firing about 5 million rounds of ammunition, using 15,000 vehicles and 1,000 helicopters. It is highly valued for military training as it has such a wide diversity of terrain, including open country, woodland, scrub and water and facilities can be provided to cope with the fast- changing needs of a modern army.

Sometimes planned changes are overtaken by events. In the late 1980s a replica German village, complete with three-storey buildings, a church and wrecked Russian tanks was built to provide for training in built-up areas. Before it was ready for use in 1990, Glasnost had swept through Europe and it was no longer needed for its original purpose. Built at a cost of £4 million and renamed 'European' village it is an anachronism, at least for the time being.

Although helicopters have been used for many years in transport-

ing troops, the formation of NATO rapid reaction forces has inten-
sified their use for deployment of troops, armoury and back-up
equipment. One exercise in 1993 is a good example of the use of the
Battle Area for this type of training. Puma and Chinook helicopters
were used to move the 24 Airmobile Brigade from barracks at
Colchester to Stanford. Two infantry battalions, 24 howitzers, med-
ical and ordnance back-up were moved 80 miles and were combat-
ready in six hours.

In the early 1990s troops were prepared for duties in Northern
Ireland. Vehicle check-points similar to those used in the Province
were built, to ensure that training could be as realistic as possible.
As the area is not used for extensive tank training, the countryside
shows very little evidence of the huge amount of military activity
which takes place.

In the vicinity of the Battle Area gunfire is often heard but is not
usually very intrusive. A large area in the centre is designated as
the impact area into which all artillery gunfire is directed. Now
that fewer troops are stationed in Europe, it is thought that maximum use will be made of the Battle Area for the foreseeable future.

Within a few years of the army taking over, most of the buildings
had been reduced to rubble and those which became unsafe had to
be demolished. Small plinths have now been installed to mark the
position of the principal ones.

Although very few buildings remain, the churches are still standing but are in a very sorry state of dereliction and decay with their
windows boarded up. The Ministry of Defence has to maintain roofs
and keep the churches watertight but beyond this necessary work,
no repairs are undertaken. The graveyards are surrounded by very
high chain-link fences. Former residents are allowed an annual visit
to the graveyards but even they are no longer allowed to go inside
the churches because of the danger of falling masonry.

As much use as possible is made of land for farming on the
fringes, consistent with military needs. Let to sixteen licensees ,
crops grown are almost entirely capable of being harvested with
combines or similar harvesters. Some cattle graze the water meadows along the River Wissey.

The most important farming activity is centred on a single flock
of 8,000 Beulah (Welsh Speckled) ewes, which had to be estab-

lished after myxomatosis had killed the rabbits and there was a danger that the open country needed by the army would progressively become scrub and, eventually, woodland. Before myxomatosis rabbits grazed so intensively that seedling trees and shrubs were destroyed.

With this massive flock of sheep, one of the largest in the country under one ownership, it was possible to manage without the need for any internal fencing. A perimeter fence had to be erected and cattle grids installed on all roads, so that movement of military vehicles was not impeded.

The sheep are managed on a heft system. Sheep in upland areas are usually managed on a similar basis. A flock becomes accustomed to grazing a particular mountain or hillside; the territorial instinct of the sheep ensures that any that go astray will eventually find their way back to their area or heft. By splitting the flock down into a number of hefts, vast movement of sheep is avoided.

When live firing is to take place, sheep are removed from the appropriate range and from the impact zone and confined in a fenced-off area where there is sufficient food until they can be released. After they are released they gradually find their way back to their heft and do not have to be driven over a long distance. Special arrangements are made during lambing, which takes place over a period of four weeks. The breed is conditioned to lambing on the open hillside and cannot be satisfactorily confined at this time. The ewes need to be quiet, undisturbed and to have more attention from the shepherd. Army training is restricted to avoid, as far as possible, the use of guns, helicopters and pyrotechnics until lambing is finished.

Since it was taken over by the army, the Battle Area, with the exception of that part used for farming and forestry, has had no pesticide applied and natural succession of plants has been allowed to occur. Habitats, typical of Breckland when it was farmed extensively, have developed and the whole area has become a haven for wildlife. It is now designated as a SSSI and is the largest lowland site under one management in this country.

Military activities do not seem to worry the wildlife. Soldiers' boots and gunfire is tolerated by birds and mammals and because there is only a limited amount of vehicular movement, other than on roads, rare plants and the insects which live on them, are relatively undisturbed. There are over 600 flower and plant species, including 28 rarities. There are 331 kinds of moths and 28 butterflies; 137 species of birds and 26 species of mammals. Wildlife is carefully monitored by a team of specialists who have permits to enter the area, consistent with army training. They compile an annual assessment of wildlife, enabling changes to be monitored. The army has the authority to over-ride conservation considerations in favour of military needs but this power is seldom exercised.

Rabbits are again so numerous that they have to be controlled in the interests of farming tenants. There are some areas where bare land around their burrows provides nesting sites for stone curlew. Other Breckland birds such as the nightjar and woodlark occur, especially after some of the woodland has been clear felled. Very large flocks of mistle thrushes are common and pied wagtails and spotted flycatchers are so numerous that nesting sites on the few buildings are well-used. Newly-erected buildings, even those of a temporary nature, are quickly colonised by birds, presumably because they are occupied so sporadically that the birds are comparatively free from human disturbance. A pair of Egyptian geese nested in an old dead tree in the early 1990s. The variety and number of birds in the area are very significant as they form a substantial reserve of native species from which other areas of Breckland can be colonised.

The River Wissey has been restocked with otters released in the late 1980s after 20 years when they had been absent. The last hunt took place in 1967 with a pack of hounds consisting of otter, stag and fox hounds. On that day within minutes of starting the hunt the stag hounds disappeared chasing a roe, the fox hounds went hotfoot after a fox and the otter hounds, it is sad to record, killed a dog otter. It took several days to find the stag and fox hounds.

Though it is unfortunate that access has to be so restricted it is reassuring to know that the wildlife benefits from the care taken of the various habitats, consistent with the Battle Area's primary use for army training.

Derelict Farmhouse, Battle Area 1977

Plinth marking site of building in Battle Area

Chapter Ten

BRECKLAND RIVERS

The Rivers Wissey, Lark and Little Ouse with its tributaries Thet and Black Bourn, all flow in an east to west direction, joining the Great Ouse in the Fens. They are classified by the National Rivers Authority as high quality 'chalk streams' and all supported otters until the 1970s. None were seen for a number of years but restocking has taken place on some stretches and this animal, which once had a stronghold in East Anglia, seems to be re-establishing itself.

All the rivers are quite small but even in the severest drought a steady flow of clear water is maintained. Formerly, this must have been of supreme importance to the many villages which are found in their valleys as water was crucial to both man and beast.

The rivers were used by early colonisers who established settlements in close proximity to use them as a means of transport, for drinking water and fish.

In the seventeenth century requests were made to Parliament to make the Lark and Ouse navigable. There was an Act of Parliament to improve navigation on the Great Ouse in 1670, and on the Lark in 1682. These dates are significant, as flows in the rivers had been adversely affected by the construction of Denver Sluice at the head of the Great Ouse in 1652. This meant that it, and its tributaries, were no longer tidal and although some navigations were improved, the Breckland rivers seem to have begun to silt up because of the reduced rate of flow in them and problems with shallow water began to arise.

To overcome the difficulty of navigating through shallow stretches of the rivers, flash-locks or staunches were introduced in the early part of the seventeenth century. A staunch had only one gate, usually suspended over the stream. To stem the flow and build up the water level upstream the gate had to lowered. It was raised or lowered with a chain on an axle turned by a big wheel with spokes which protruded about half a metre beyond its circumference. The protruding parts of the spokes were used to tread on, in treadmill fashion to turn the wheel.

Staunches were introduced because they were relatively cheap to construct but they had a number of disadvantages, including the waste of water and the long delays which they imposed on river transport. If the gate was down when a barge approached proceeding upstream, it had to be raised. The barge then had to be pulled up against a strong current of water. The task would sometimes be too great for the hauling horse and a system of winches had to be used. Having gone through, the barge was moored while the gate was lowered, and then it had to wait until the water level had built up sufficiently for it to be able to proceed. Long delays could ensue as sometimes the water level had to be raised over a stretch of several kilometres.

A barge going downstream had different problems. If there was insufficient water, a man on horseback rode to the next staunch

The Little Ouse near Santon Downham

downstream to close it down. When the barge eventually reached the staunch it was swept through when the water was released by raising the gate. This was a dangerous operation and occasionally men and horses were pulled into the water by the force of the current.

Whilst the staunches made navigation possible, the delays caused could be considerable. It is estimated that under adverse conditions a barge would proceed only three to four kilometres a day when water was low and staunches had to be used, as compared with 25 to 30 kilometres on open stretches of river where there was no obstruction. Remains of staunches can be seen at both St Helen's picnic site at Santon and at West Stow Country Park.

The defects of staunches were overcome with the introduction of pound locks in the eighteenth century. A pound lock has two gates which allows relatively quick and smooth passage using comparatively little water. Operating this type of lock is quite simple although sometimes arduous depending on the design of the gates and winding gear. A barge going downstream enters the lock when it is full of water. The gate behind the barge is then closed and water is discharged from the lock by opening the paddles in the forward gate. Gradually the lock empties until the water is at the new lower level of the river and the barge is able to proceed through the open forward gate. Operating the lock takes some time, especially when it is set in the opposite position to which the barge is travelling. Nevertheless, the procedure avoids the problems of flushing-through experienced with staunches, and the water level of the river is reasonably constant so that, once through a lock, a craft can continue its journey immediately.

There are disused locks at Mildenhall on the Lark and the remains of the unusually interesting Cherry Ground lock at West Stow Country Park, which is about seven kilometres downstream from Bury St. Edmunds. The majority of pound locks were constructed to be just wide and long enough to take craft using the navigation. This minimises the amount of water used each time the lock is operated and consequently also minimises the time for filling and emptying it. At West Stow the lock is crescent shaped and obviously far wider and longer than would appear to be necessary. Since craft on these rivers were usually moved in gangs of two or more, it might have been possible to get the gang into this lock which then would have saved water and reduced the delay to the journey. The site of the lock-keeper's cottage, built in 1842, is marked at West Stow and is surprisingly distant from the crescent lock which was not constructed until 1892. It seems possible that there was a lock close by the cottage, which was replaced later by the crescent lock.

Under normal conditions the three Breckland rivers still flow into the Great Ouse as they have for centuries past. After the disastrous floods of 1947, and a review of water control in the South Level of the Fens, extensive new works were authorised by the Great Ouse River Flood Protection Act in 1949. As part of the scheme which was completed in 1964, a cut-off channel was dug to the east of Breckland. It starts near Barton Mills, runs beside the A1065 at Mildenhall Wood, skirts Lakenheath, Hockwold and Feltwell, and eventually ends at Denver.

As a result of this scheme, flood water from the rivers can be diverted via syphons directly into the cut-off channel, thus reducing the risk of flooding in the Fens. Water from the Great Ouse can be made to flow back along the cut-off channel as far as Hockwold, where it enters a tunnel to be eventually discharged into the Rivers Stour, Colne and Blackwater to help to maintain water levels in some of the Essex reservoirs. The total distance of transfer from Denver to Abberton Reservoir is 141 kilometres and to Hanningfield 148 kilometres.

There is no remaining description of the river craft which traded along the rivers in the fifteenth and sixteenth centuries, but it is probable they were small and of shallow draught. A number of fenland villages had wharfs and hythes and it could be that goods were off-loaded on to larger barges for the passage to Wisbech or Cambridge.

After the major fenland drainage schemes in the seventeenth century, and improvements to navigation on the Breckland rivers, barges were able to move over the full extent of the waterways without hindrance, other than any resulting from the staunches. Fen barges or lighters which used the rivers were worked in gangs of four. Each barge was sixteen metres long with a beam of three metres. When empty they took less than one metre of water and when fully laden with 25 tonnes, about one and a half metres were needed.

During the Middle Ages, a very wide range of goods was carried for local use. The Bishop of Ely moved produce from his Breckland estates to Ely on a regular basis. Wool from Suffolk, much of it handled by merchants in the Bury St. Edmunds area, was shipped for export via King's Lynn. In the early years of the nineteenth century the River Lark was known as the 'coal river' because of the volume of this commodity being carried. Water was particularly valuable for carrying heavy goods such as bricks when roads were inadequate, even for slow moving waggons.

Comparatively large numbers of horses were needed to pull the gangs of barges. They had to be stabled and fed and the lightermen were catered for by riverside inns. Each regular had a slate on which was recorded his beer consumption in pints (Ps) and quarts (Qs) for which he paid periodically. This was the origin of 'Mind your Ps and Qs' as a warning to watch the bill which was building up for the day of reckoning.

Tolls were levied at various places along the rivers. The money went to the owner of the toll rights but net profits were usually very low because of the heavy expense incurred for the maintenance of the navigation. Tolls on the River Lark rose from £1,348 in 1807 to £1,639 in 1818, but over a similar period expenses rose from £633 in 1812 to £1,154 in 1817. In 1817 eighty commissioners were appointed to supervise the navigational rights but by 1843 it was necessary to appoint another fifty 'to fill vacancies occasioned by death'. The middle of the nineteenth century must have been a very worrying time as the railways were reaching out in all directions.

In 1844 several barges were still working between Brandon and King's Lynn carrying coal, corn and timber and there was a regular service twice weekly. At the same time, there were barges daily from Mildenhall to Bury St. Edmunds and King's Lynn. In 1845 at Thetford, the imports by water included coal and timber, and exports were listed as corn, wool and other agricultural produce; there was still a weekly service to King's Lynn. The Great Eastern Railway Company completed its line between London and Norwich, via Brandon and Thetford in 1845, and introduced fierce competition to the commercial river traffic, which went into a slow terminal decline after the arrival of the railways.

Prince Duleep Singh acquired the estates in the Lakenheath area in 1863 and about ten years later began to redevelop the sand and gravel pits on Lakenheath Warren. His aim was to move as much as possible by barge and to facilitate this, restored the old wharf at Lakenheath and had the river dredged out. As late as 1900, 25-30 tonne barges were leaving the wharf twice weekly. A single horse could pull three barges and there was no other way of moving such quantities due to the inadequate fenland roads.

There was a slight revival of barge traffic with the completion of the beet sugar factories at Ely and Wissington in 1925. Barges carrying beet operated from Lakenheath but only penetrated as far as Prickwillow on the River Lark and to Stoke Ferry on the River Wissey, so had very little effect on the Breckland sections of these rivers.

The rivers are now used to a limited extent for leisure craft but some sections are very popular with canoeists.

Entrance to the Maze, High Lodge

Chapter Eleven

PLACES TO VISIT

Barnham Cross Common. A local Nature Reserve. South of Thetford on either side of A134. Grassland, heath and scrub. TL 865814

Brandon, Heritage Centre. In George Street. Displays tracing the history of flint mining and knapping; the rabbit and fur industry, forestry and local interest section. Housed in former fire station premises.

Brandon, Country Park. The landscaped grounds with a lake and woodland around the 1826 Brandon Park House (a private hotel) are open to the public. Visitor Centre with excellent information displays about Breckland natural habitats. Victorian walled garden has wonderful flower beds of both cultivated and wild species. Woodland picnic areas. Forest walks. Toilets. TL 785854

Bury St. Edmunds. Moyses Hall Museum. Cornhill at the corner of the Market Place. Bury's oldest building, this was a twelfth century merchant's house with living room above the vaulted undercroft. Now an excellent local museum, includes many artifacts from the Anglo-Saxon village of Stowa at West Stow.

Cavenham Heath. English Nature. Areas of grassland, heath and birch woodland. Many Breckland birds and plants. Area of heath with numerous rabbits. Access only to area south of the Tuddenham - Icklingham road. Car park at Temple Bridge near River Lark. This bridge is steep and narrow and the approach from Tuddenham is preferred by many visitors. TL 758729

Croxton. Devil's Punchbowl. Forestry Commission land with picnic area and forest walks. Breckland mere with fluctuating water level. Dry in 1992-93. TL 878892

East Wretham Heath. Norfolk Naturalists Trust. Typical Breckland, includes areas of open heath and grassland, as well as Langmere and Ringmere. Supports a rich variety of flowers and birds, as well as adders! A beautiful stand of pines planted just after the Battle of Waterloo in 1815. The nature trail includes a section for the visually handicapped. TL 913887

Godwick. English Heritage. Deserted village. Between Tittleshall and Whissonsett, just outside of Breckland. The only example of a deserted village with public access nearby. TF 903223

Knettishall Heath. Suffolk County Council. Its habitats include heath, open grassland and mixed woodland. Remains of rabbit warren and round barrows. Way-marked walks. Both the Peddars Way and Angles Way can be joined from here. Car park. Picnic area. Toilets. TL 956806

Lynford. Arboretum. Forestry Commission. Over 100 species of conifers and broad-leaved trees both in plots and as individual specimens. Especially attractive in the spring when daffodils are in flower. Pleasant walks around the arboretum, lake, sequoia avenue and adjoining forest. TL 821941

Lynford. Grimes Graves. English Heritage. Site of Neolithic flint mines 4,000 years old. First excavated in the 1870s. One pit open to visitors. Visitor centre with displays of history of flint mining. Surrounded by open heathland with brilliant covering of flowers in spring and summer. TL 818898

Lynford Stag. The centre piece is a metal stag bearing the inscription 'The target stag was used by Sir Richard Sutton for shooting practice. He was a former owner of nearby Lynford Hall, and an eminent Master of Foxhounds and skilled shot of his time'. The stag was found by Forestry Commission employees when the area was afforested in the 1930s. Car park, play area, forest walks and toilets. TL 812919

Mildenhall and District Museum. King Street. Local voluntary museum in early nineteenth century cottages. Displays on local archaeology, RAF Mildenhall, Breckland and Fenland.

Santon Downham. The Forest District Office, administrative centre of the Forest Park. Bird trail, through Santon Valley Forest Nature Reserve to St Helen's picnic area (also approached by road) along the River Little Ouse. Car Park, toilets. TL 815878

Thetford. Ancient House Museum. White Hart Street. This half-timbered building dates from 1500 and has especially fine carved ceilings. Displays on local history, flint, archaeology and natural history. Also local Tourist Information Centre. TL 873829

Thetford. The Charles Burrell Museum. Minstergate. History of world famous company 1770 to 1932. Main features include steam engines and agricultural machinery. Housed in former Burrell paint-finishing shop.

Thetford Forest Park. Britain's largest lowland pine forest. Access points, car parks, picnic sites and way- marked paths throughout the area. See also Santon Downham.

High Lodge Forest Centre. Off B1107 near Brandon. Leisure centre of Forest Enterprise. Walks, cycle trails (cycles can be hired), children's play area, wildlife hide, forest drive, shop, refreshments, toilets. Special events are arranged during the summer. TL 810851

Thetford Warren Lodge and Rishbeth Wood. Remains of the fifteenth century two-storey house built for the warrener and his family. Three way-marked routes in Rishbeth Wood. Trim Trail with 10 exercise points. District Council car park adjacent to the B1107 Thetford to Brandon road. TL 839841

Thompson Common. Norfolk Naturalists Trust. Open grassland

and woodland, numerous pingos. Great Eastern Pingo trail (Norfolk Country Council) starts at Stow Bedon station. Walk links with Peddars Way, round Thompson Water. Trail follows disused railway line. TL 934967

Weeting Castle. English Heritage. Remains of a twelfth century fortified manor house standing within a dry moat. Ice house. TL 768891

Weeting Heath. Norfolk Naturalists Trust. Bird hides. Stone curlews and wheatears nest on the heath. Heathland flowers. TL 934967

West Stow, Anglo-Saxon village and Country Park. Suffolk County Council. A reconstruction of the village of Stowa from evidence provided by archaeological excavations. Visitor centre contains interpretive displays about the site. Taped guides, with sound effects and music, bring the village to life. Nature trail across park along River Lark and lakes. Toilets, picnic area and children's playground. TL 795715

West Stow. King's Forest. Special plantings for Silver Jubilee of King George V and Queen Mary, 1935, one of which is Queen Mary's avenue of beech, close to the Icknield Way. Two way-marked walks from car park on B1106 between Bury St. Edmunds and Elveden. TL 825749

Peddars Way. Long-distance footpath from Knettishall to Holme-next-the-Sea where it joins the Norfolk coastal path.

Icknield Way. Long-distance track crosses Breckland from Newmarket to Holme-next-the-Sea.